HOW TO ADVERTISE ON FACEBOOK

A 2020 Guide to Generate High Ticket Sales from Facebook Leads. A-Z Strategy to Grow Your Online Business

By Jim Norton

publisher for any reparation, damages, or monetary loss due to the information herein, either directly or indirectly.

Respective authors own all copyrights not held by the publisher.

The information herein is offered for informational purposes solely and is universal as so. The presentation of the information is without a contract or any type of guarantee assurance. The trademarks that are used are without any consent, and the publication of the trademark is without permission or backing by the trademark owner. All trademarks and brands within this book are for clarifying purposes only and are owned by the owners themselves, not affiliated with this document.

DISCLAIMER

FOREWORD

First, I will like to thank you for taking the first step of trusting me and deciding to purchase/read this life-transforming eBook. Thanks for spending your time and resources on this material. I can assure you of the exact blueprint I lay bare in the information manual you are currently reading. It has transformed lives, and I strongly believe it will equally transform your life too. All the information I presented in this Do-It-Yourself is easy to digest and practice.

Table of Contents

CHAPTER ONE: Why Advertise on Facebook: The Pros and Pros 10

CHAPTER TWO: Marketing and the Facebook Revolution . 14

CHAPTER THREE: Key Performance Indicators (KPIs) 44

CHAPTER FOUR: Designing your Ads 77

CHAPTER FIVE: Facebook's Powerful Targeting 81

CHAPTER SIX: Campaigns, Pricing, and Scheduling 128

CHAPTER SEVEN: Facebook Ads Finances 132

CHAPTER EIGHT: Facebook Advertising Hacks to Generate High-Ticket Sales 152

CHAPTER NINE: Landing Page Considerations...............165

CHAPTER TEN: Dynamic Landing Pages, Tagging, and Conversion Tracking 172

INTRODUCTION

The growth of social networking sites has also reached an exponential level, along with the increasing competition in the online marketing industry. With social networking sites like Facebook and Twitter consuming a large part of the daily lives of internet users worldwide, it will only be a matter of time when online marketing strategies make their way to these social networking sites.

Facebook is actually one of the internet's most popular social networking websites, with more than 5 million members worldwide. Tap into that young internet user population and you have yourself an instant source of millions of prospects and target audiences.

That's why most of the online businesses these days are starting to enter the Facebook market, as well as various organizations that want to sell their brand online. The interesting thing about Facebook is that most of the units on the website are non-traditional and are often mixed with a specific type of content that engages users whenever they log in-basically the kind of information that appears on their Facebook feeds.

The main reason a lot of advertisers are beginning to get through Facebook's mighty walls is its massive user volume. Facebook is nothing more than a very large networking site that offers a great opportunity for the granular targeting-the website itself already has enough user supplies that will allow online advertisers and marketers to put in a bunch of campaigns.

And because Facebook is a website where people from all over the world openly share some details about themselves, it is really easy for online marketers and advertisers to narrow down their goals. State, state, city, age, gender, interests, relationship status, employment, music, profile keywords, and books are often targeting factors.

There are a number of ways of advertising and breaking into the Facebook business. Depending on the type of business you have, and your target audience, there is at least one Facebook platform that will allow you to promote your products and services.

• The Facebook Page

You can create a profile for your business, brand, company or even for your products or services using the Facebook Page Facebook pages. For promotional purposes, other non-profit organizations and groups such as bands, public figures, and artists may also have a Facebook page.

Having a Facebook page will give you the opportunity to socialize with other Facebook users while at the same time gaining mark affinity and building brand relationships.

• Facebook ads

Running a Facebook ad can come in a variety of forms-as a sponsored story, sponsored social story, video sponsor story, or a pure display ad. Facebook ads are suitable for short, succinct online advertising of a particular brand or service.

It seems as if these days everyone has a Facebook page and that isn't far from the truth. There are millions of Facebook users worldwide and the social networking website continues to grow at an accelerated rate. Because of this, Facebook advertising has been caught on by business owners and they have realized how easy it is to reach their target demographic of people using Facebook advertising.

Facebook advertising, like any other form of advertising, does cost money. This could lead some business owners to shy away from using this form of marketing because they do not want to spend the money. Fortunately, there are a few different ways to make cheap savings and advertisements on Facebook.

The first thing to remember about Facebook advertising is that no matter how much or how little money you spend, the key is getting people to click on the ad. One of the easiest ways of doing that is to insert an image or illustration into the commercial. This will make the commercial more appealing to the viewer and will also help make it stand out better. Write out the words for the text portion of the ad, so that it is easy for the user to tell what they will get if they click on the ad. Users like to be accurate and to the point, so if the ad rambles about a lot of nothing, it may not get clicked on.

Now that you know a few tips on what your ads will contain on Facebook, here are a few tips on cheap advertising:

• When you market an online business, make sure to use keywords that apply to the website you market. It's fun to play around with ad campaigns and come up with some creative ads, but if the ads aren't relevant to the website, the money will be wasted.

• If you have a local business or are only interested in targeting Facebook users from certain countries or localities, please ensure that information is input when setting up the campaign. When appealing to all users a lot of money is spent on Facebook ads, instead of just the people who are interested in a product or service being offered.

• Setting the maximum cost per click very low is one of the best ways to advertise cheaply on Facebook. Facebook has a habit of setting it high but you don't have to pay the Facebook lists pre-filled amount.

If you're one of 62 million Facebook users, you're aware of what the site's become a networking force! The thought of 62 million potential customers should make you drool with anticipation if you're a business owner. The question is, how does a business owner use an advertising message to reach Facebook subscribers? The article will highlight crucial approaches to Facebook ads.

Many marketers stay away from Facebook because the site has many 18-25 age group subscribers. I say, "so what?" There's still plenty of users in every age group to make Facebook ads more than worthwhile. What's more, the 18-25-year-old subscribers are also consumers.

There are several valuable promotional tools available on the web. Advertisers can buy banner ads, and use flyers targeting specific groups. Such flyers are on the website, and can be purchased for as little as 5.oo! You can insert in your homepage a resource called "Next Move," with links to similar supported groups. Quite realistic! One may also place ads within the news feeds of their homepage. The "notes" segment is a great way to send messages. Acting almost like a blog, the message is sent to all the news feeds your friend gets when you write something on it.

The real key to Facebook ads is through word of mouth. Studies have reiterated the fact that people are 3-4 times more likely to buy an item from a person they know. Enter communities to which your product or service is linked. If you are selling travel packages, join a group you love to travel. Join groups that focus on your interests and passions. Upon initial contact with your group members, get to know them on a personal level before you approach them on a business level. See if you can do them a profit. SOCIAL! Introduce your product or service in such a way that you are not "pushing it" after you get to know them. A great approach is to ask for help in introducing your product or service to people in other groupings. If you get to know and apply this approach regularly with several people in your groups, word of mouth advertising for your product or service will be "snowball."A great addition to this word of mouth approach is forming a group yourself. You will gain almost immediate leadership status and there will be dramatically increased respect for your product or service.

Thousands of articles and posts online will be seen and read telling you that Facebook is one of the best ways to sell and promote your product online. While most of those articles speak about the free process, the social networking site actually has something more to give than free but not guaranteed publicity. Therefore, we are led to the idea that if you are trying to get the advantage you've always wanted toward online competition, there may be advertisement costs on Facebook.

So what is the quality of Facebook advertising? Let's find out: The answer is not really as clear as you might have expected in fact. Giving a specific number is actually difficult because the response will rely greatly on the competition. It means that if there are a large number of online marketers and companies targeting the same market and demographics as you do, usually the cost is higher. But if you're alone, it becomes a lot cheaper to advertise on Facebook.

But then again, if the cost is too big to bear you can't just lose hope. In fact, there's a way to get you going around it and being clever enough. This can be done if you are well aware of the workings and activities of the social networking site. Note that marketing and advertising on Facebook are likely to correlate with very good investment returns. Before running for that much-needed internet marketing campaign, though, there are certain things you need to know and understand.

For general, Facebook ads offer you two choices for a cost model. The first is what's called Cost per Tap and the second is the Cost per Thousand Impressions.

What are the variations, and what are those two? So here's a quick look for both and a reference.

The first one, CPC, includes you having to pay the moment someone clicks on the ad. CPM, on the other hand, means you're going to pay as soon as a thousand people see the commercial. There is an auction system in both schemes, or more like an Auction. The cost of ads on Facebook, in this case, would depend greatly on what other advertisers are willing to pay for either the clicks or views using or under the same demographics.

It should be noted that in areas or places where competition among advertisers is so intense on the same demographics, which is characterized by criteria such as gender, age, region, and others, the costs are most likely to be higher.

Finally, if you are really interested in making your company thrive online in no time, the cost of ads on Facebook could be just a minor concern for you. Social media marketing and Facebook advertising are the same as others, so you'll need to try and test every possible method to come up with what's really perfect for your business niche. But as a friendly guide, it's important to remember that CPC will result in higher click-through-rate while CPM produces fewer links but in general they are relatively cheaper.

CHAPTER ONE

Why Advertise on Facebook: The Pros and Pros

I know. I know. I know. You may think the title has "Why to Advertise on Facebook: The Pros and Cons" typo errors But, it's correct and deliberately written that way, because when it comes to advertising on social networking giant Facebook, there aren't really "cons." Okay, perhaps there is, but the "cons" are far too tiny to be significant.

Why Facebook advertisements?

This is the most common issue among advertisers and even some of those successful marketing firms that use traditional search engines, Google or direct mail, and owners of small businesses. The list below will help you to ponder why Facebook advertising is different and more profitable compared to traditional advertising methods.

1. Especially for small companies, it has a great advantage, because they can make their business accessible to the public even without spending a lot of money like what successful businesses do.

2. For Facebook, the audience is the whole globe.

3. It has new insights on Facebook where you can see who those users are and how many like your Facebook fan page.

4. Socially and professionally accessing your customers is very easy, while talking about what your product is all about.

5 You pay less to do a big promotion for your brand or business.

6. Customers can get their answers directly from the advertisers or the company's owner right away from their queries.

7. Advertisers who have spent a lot of money on advertising can maximize their budget and optimize it by advertising their own brand on Facebook.

8. Social networks like Facebook are less expensive when it comes to advertising than traditional advertising.

9. Facebook will give you the luxury of making your marketing plan or advertising ads imaginative and inventive.

10. Facebook is a mixed environment. It enables everyone to interact or reconnect, socialize, talk and share whatever people are interested in. Mouthword is strong and Facebook is the new word for mouth.

These are still many more advantages, just to answer why Facebook advertises. It's a big, opportunities and activities world. In fact, Facebook connects more than just people to people, it also connects:

• People to a social group of individuals

• people to organizations

• people to education

• people to schools

• people to brands

• people to interest and hobbies

• people to events

• people to business enterprises, etc.

There is no need to spend a lot of money advertising on expensive online advertising company. In reality, in the field of advertising, there are companies that have a great reputation but the feedback and comments are not trustworthy.

All you need to do is have an appealing, insightful and well-updated Facebook advertising, and be sure to take a look at the important issues that need to be addressed especially when it comes to customer queries. Keep your products and services clear and trustworthy; however successful they may be, if you can not build a strong and trustworthy relationship with your customers, you will be thrown in the garbage. Remember that you advertise on Facebook; that's increasing revenue and getting more buyers, and that's where your customers come from.

CHAPTER TWO

Marketing and the Facebook Revolution

Facebook has culled, unofficially, more than 700 million users around the world since its launch nearly seven years ago. The largest social networking website has penetrated pop culture with sitcom quotes and even their own feature-length movie. "Like us on Facebook" has become almost popular vernacular in both local and corporate brands. This chapter will take you through a high-level look at Facebook, from its unassuming development in a dormitory room in Harvard to the basic dos and don'ts for social marketers.

The rapid rise, absolute domination, user-base girth, global reach and sheer marketing power of Facebook's Scope Facebook is staggering— a true contextual marketing paradigm-buster. More than half of Facebook's officially revealed 500 million users sign in each day, participating for an aggregate of 700 billion minutes per month, according to Facebook's released figures as from this writing. That's right, 700 bn.

"Facebook" was the top search term for the second straight year in 2010 according to Experian Hitwise. Measured by Google's own tool, Insights for Search, Facebook search interest is a fanatical, fading search buzz for Google worldwide.

More than 900 million profiles, communities, gatherings, and community accounts have been accumulated on the social networking site. Users generate more than 30 billion monthly Web links, news stories, blog posts, notes, photo albums, and other blocks of shared content. Because about 70 percent of users come from outside the United States, a virtual army of 300,000 volunteers is using the Translations app to translate content.

Currently, two hundred and fifty million on-the-go mobile users access Facebook via their cell phones, iPads and other devices. More than a million business people and developers from 190 countries produced over half a billion applications. Since the launch of social plugins in April 2010 an average of 10,000 new websites have been integrated with Facebook every day. More than 2.5 million websites have been integrated with Facebook, including more than 80 of the United States comScore. Top 100 blogs, and more than half the World Top 100 comScore.

The rise to power of Facebook was as appallingly swift and, in a way, as prodigal as its eccentric, youthful brain trust. A group of four now-infamous Harvard students led by Mark Zuckerberg, who was a computer science student and brilliant hacker with a website scraping gift for black hat and a deep intuition of human social motivations founded the social network. In February 2004, Zuckerberg and co-founders Dustin Moskovitz, Chris Hughes, and Eduardo Saverin launched Facebook from their Harvard dorm room (then known as "The Web"). By March of that year, the site, previously an exclusive online Harvard-only network, expanded to include students from Columbia, Stanford and Yale. In June, the Facebook crew moved to Palo Alto, California where the staple profile features of Facebook Groups and the distinguishing Wall were added. In December, the upstart social network celebrated reaching the 1-million active-user mark — incredibly, less than a year after launch. It was obvious that the Facebook revolution was seriously underway now.

In May 2005, Accel Partners raised $12.7 million in venture capital from the relocated Bay Area startup, and by August more than 800 colleges and universities grew into an envelope. Students fell in love with the heady mix of community, dating, college play, and friendships found on Facebook. Zuckerberg was proving himself to be a freakishly genius wizard of the new online virtual pheromones crucible for a guy with a serious nerd rap.

Things really began to heat up in September when Facebook started to allow high school students around the country to create accounts. The web Photos core was launched in October, at which point the platform also began assimilating international school networks. By December 2005, the user base had grown to include over 5.5 million active users by an astounding 500 percent. It was obvious that Zuckerberg was getting his finger on the pounding pulse of new social media on the Internet. Facebook raised plenty of eyebrows, though far from common, mainly from advertisers asking where this would lead. By then, clever marketers have among other things been finding ways to gain access to college accounts to test word-of-mouth marketing. At this time, Facebook was particularly fertile because college kids had no idea whatsoever that marketers are in the mix.

Facebook opened the once ivy-clad walled garden even more in 2006, another year of astronomical growth, providing free registration for anyone who wishes to join. The future king of social networks was poised to explode into international sharing of mind no longer strictly for students. Greylock Partners and Meritech Capital Partners invested $27.5 million to keep things scaling. Further apps have been introduced including the Notes app, the now omnipresent News Feed, Mini-Feed, the Development Platform, new privacy controls, and sharing functionality. Facebook and Microsoft joined a strategic alliance to serve ads on syndicated banners. By December, the user base had been expanding to 12 million people internationally. The user base's volume and diversity had merchants salivating. Many of us were wondering what the FB crew had up their sleeves to make advertisers accessible to the community members.

In April 2007, the global Facebook network had 20 million active users, attracting more than 2 million Canadians and 1 million active UK users of all ages and stripes. But changes of seismic proportions that would eventually shake the known Internet universe right up to the end of the first decade of the millennium were to come that year. Facebook was ready to move beyond the "website" status to become an "operating system," which eventually set the stage for Facebook ads.

The new Facebook Platform was unveiled on May 24, 2007 during the San Francisco f8 Event. An official press release read, "Facebook, the leading social utility on the Internet, today announced that more than 65 developer partners have developed applications on Facebook Platform, a new development platform that allows businesses and engineers to integrate into the Facebook network and reach millions of users." Although marketers were still wondering what was for them on Facebook, the approach to the platform was a huge factor in attracting users who make up today's Facebook Ads targeting pool.

In short, Microsoft took an equity stake in Facebook of $240 million and cut off an international advertising partnership deal. Marketers asked what this meant. Would there be a do-it-yourself

(DIY) ad platform or would media purchases on Facebook be limited to buying Microsoft banners forever? Google's Content Network enabled us to access certain Facebook pages but marketers wanted more. We wondered what was to come next. So Facebook launched its new mobile platform and mushroomed the network in size to an unprecedented 50 million active users. Marketers were thinking, "Those users are all good. When will we get actual access? "Then, when Facebook Ads was born in November, the marketing tsunami hit a vengeance. This was a mind-bending breakthrough for a relatively small group of conscientious online marketers— Facebook's rapidly expanding user base was now readily accessible to any advertiser in sleek DIY design. It was amazing— instead of marketing to search for the keyword "audio recording college Minnesota," marketers were able to target high school guys who were interested in playing guitar, were single, or possibly played in a band. As they say, the rest is history. The gold standard in contextual online marketing was born.

It was important to understand the evolving demographics of the early adoption of Facebook Ads marketers. Failure to do so meant that a lot of search marketers failed early. At the time, Facebook was still somewhat skewed towards college students, of course, as they have been there from the start. Speaking at Search Engine Strategies New York 2008, I preached to a crowd that scarcely cared about the "imminent social PPC revolution."

goClear, previously skilled in segmenting landing pages based on inbound search queries, began creating marketing landing page variations to inbound gender, age, interests, relationship status, and other highly personal attributes.

In January 2008, Facebook took a dramatically progressive turn to co-sponsor the presidential debates in conjunction with ABC News. Friend list privacy controls were put in place alongside a 21-language translation program on the heels of launch in Spanish, French, and German. Chat was released and the next landmark was reached: Without looking back, Facebook blew across the 100 million-user mark.

As of Christmas Eve 2009, Facebook gained 7.56 percent of the U.S. Internet traffic market share compared to Google's 7.56 percent Several key developments in 2009 woven Facebook into the human media and cultural fabric. First, CNN Live incorporated Facebook into its online product, and at the same time, a major advertising effort was made on live cable newscasts. The Like feature was introduced, and Facebook was then valued at an unprecedented $10 billion after Digital Sky Technologies paid $200 million for preferred stock. Launched Facebook usernames which messed directly (and perhaps deliberately) with Google, Yahoo!and Bing; usernames meant that pages and person profiles were more likely to index keywords and names in the Facebook titles in organic search engine results. It also allowed "vanity" URLs, like Facebook.com / mashable or Facebook.com / MartyWeintraub. Facebook has counted a whopping 350 million users after the purchase of FriendFeed.

We were witnessing the launch in 2010 of two internal applications: Questions and Places. Things are still growing at an incredible pace; Facebook is the most visited website in the United States, blowing out of the water the nearest social media contender, YouTube, with more than a 3:1 ratio and more than 3 percent more traffic than Google's second contender.

This much is clear: From the playfully mischievous practices of a data-scraping dorm-room IT prankster, Facebook has evolved into the global social media gold standard in the six and a half years since its inception. Mark Zuckerberg is both revered and reviled, and has a net worth of about $6.9 billion, according to his July 2010 profile in Forbes magazine— not bad for a 26-year-old White Plains, New York hacker. It is estimated that Facebook itself is worth about $70 billion, of which "Zuck" reportedly owns 24 percent. His hard-driven vision of a social product, design, service, the development of core technology, human nature, and open-source infrastructure has proved both prescient and remarkable.

Understanding the Social Graph The idea of monitoring the characteristics that characterize a person is nothing new. The

French sociologist David Émile Durkheim (1858–1917) wrote of a "mechanical solidarity" that wins when personality differences are bridged, and of an "organic solidarity" that takes on independent positions when distinct individuals collaborate.

Floyd Henry Allport and Gordon Willard Allport have methodically made their hand-sketched "social maps" in their book of 1921, Personality Traits: Their Identification and Measurement, to perform vivid research on 11 nodes of human behavior.

Mark Zuckerberg is widely accredited for applying this concept in name to social media online. The designation appears fitting. Of course, in today's data-driven environment, individuals can be reduced to a list of personal affinities, at least to a considerable extent.

The term social graph these days refers to the matrix of interests and personal inclinations of Facebook which make each person unique in their meanderings. The inimitable footprint of each Facebook user is "graphed" and then stored in the centralized database on the internet. These captured personality traits make up the targeting grid — Facebook sells the "inventory" to advertisers.

Facebook tracks known and unrevealed user participation

variables in order to create its social graph. As with Google's storied organic search results ranking algorithm, marketers can only guess at any number of "black box" graph variables. This tuned combination of social graph data points represents the secret sauce behind Facebook Ads. The algorithmic lattice, in all probability, often develops in subtle ways without Facebook corporate announcement or fanfare.

Note: The social graph refers to a grid of identification of interests and personal tendencies that make individuals unique.

The easiest to understand social graph data points are the ones on Facebook ads that target the UI. In terms of marketers ' ability to target users for ads, the base targeting attributes, basically data points on the social graph, are groundbreaking. Sex, geographic location, age, sexual preference, relationship status, workplace and attributes of education combine to be very strong. As an example of targeting range, the social graph attributes to married male graduates in Criminal Justice and Criminology, who work in various police departments around the United States, who are 24 to 55 years old.

Targeting Facebook Ads requires an attribute called "Precise Interests," which is reported only sparsely, despite its omnipresent scope. The inline support in the ad creation tool offers only a brief description of what targeted "Precise Interest" entails.

You have to search through the FB help pages to really get a feel for what parts of user-profiles are being taken out to include the Precise Interests and available for social graph targeting. Here's how Facebook explains to advertisers Precise Interests in the Facebook Ads Help section "Likes & Interests Targeting." "Likes & Interests targeting helps you to tailor the target audience of your ad based on the content they have included in their profiles, as well as the Sites, Groups and other on-site material they have chosen to link to. This covers areas such as Interests, Sports, Favorite Music, Films, and TV Shows. This gives us a better idea of what aspects we can access through the Precise Interests of a person.

Let's get a bit more poking around. In, "Why do I see the specific ads that I see on Facebook? Support offered users curious about the advertising they're watching, here's how FB describes ad targeting:' Facebook ads that target your venue, sex, age, relationship status, professional or educational background, or interests you've mentioned in your profile and the pages and groups you're connected to... (OK, we know all that, but here's the major BlackBox kicker)... including more information about your professional.

"More material relating to the interests?" May the relevance improve?" What does that mean? Basically FB tells users that the big black box could include any aspect of their daily meanderings, profile information or whatever. What do marketers mean by that? For now, just keep in mind that FB doesn't tell us everything to do with users that might impact targeting, and there are amazing insights for users to exploit and mine.

Facebook's genius is that the core features mirror types of social activities that are commonly shared by humans. The term viral is often applied to the social media trend. Facebook is the epitome of virility online in that apps encourage and reinforce persuasive activities in which humans take part in physical life. People love sending photos to their families, reaching out to make new friends, contributing to critical day-to-day conversations, discussing mutual interests and exchanging material that matters to individuals and social groups. We listen to music, do jobs, watch TV and read books. The social network keeps track, quietly recording our personal predilections as we articulate them and providing the highest bidders with pieces from us.

Think about it: sharing pictures with your mom in those seemingly forever-ago pre-Internet days meant getting extra prints, stuffing them in an envelope that you'd need to address, stamp, mail and wait for her to receive. Making friends meant going through the room to physical events and seeing someone, followed by first openings and getting to know each other. Facebook provides amazing tools to simplify these, as well as many other universal activities and indulgences. (The fact that dabbling in voyeurism and different levels of anonymity is socially acceptable to users seems to make the experience all the more enchanting.) Facebook pushes human buttons around interactions, relationships, news, activities, community congregations, etc. to cater to the fundamentally primitive aspects of being an individual, making it easier to communicate than in the physical world. It is no wonder that this is such a powerful marketing tool. People love Facebook for how it streamlines so much of what's important for social people.

Facebook's "quality" charges users in return for the "free" use of these millennial resources that come with the revealing data from our behavior. Blindly, users abandon their data for free. There are no privacy settings for turning off the internal Facebook data mining for Facebook ads. Facebook's social graph, the core of Facebook's demographic targeting, is perhaps the biggest marketing development since the search.

What Marketers Can and Can't Do With Facebook

Ads consumers can't turn off Facebook Ads and FB doesn't record how targeting is influenced by privacy settings if any. Our testing indicates that locking down privacy settings to the maximum permitted protection does not prevent targeted user attributes. That's really exciting news for advertisers. Even in the light of the ongoing debate on privacy and "Do not track" initiatives, I just sleep well at night knowing that users we aim to sign off on Facebook's privacy policies in exchange for using free Facebook tools. One thing is certain: the fewer privacy users have, the more money Facebook would raise from advertisers and the more marketers can use user information to sell things! Facebook's main apps have the ability to ooze loads of user's information. Basically, only Facebook knows all the details of the Facebook activities of users that appear in algorithm-targeted corners of the FB Ads. When users don't want Facebook marketers to approach them, the best answer is to close their accounts.

Facebook Ads Terms of Services

At the end of the day, it's getting ads approved, up and running that matters most to marketers. The best way to know if you have violated Terms of Service (TOS) is to disapprove of an ad coming back. Facebook's terms of service are an interesting potpourri of rules that restrict marketers from selling certain items, impose stipulations around others, and outright ban different technical and promotional tactics. There are some rules which are common sense. Others were added in response to various spammer ploys over the years.

It's important to note that since the program relies on people exercising editorial control, it isn't always even applying the rules.

We have been running ads successfully for weeks on many occasions and cloned them to change the pictures only to have the almost duplicate ad rejected. If an ad you submit does not appear to violate any identifiable item in the terms of the service list, then simply re-send it.

Here is a partial list of what is not permitted; if in doubt, always refer to the new FB Advertising Guidelines contained in the help section: Automated advertising without authorization.

Announcements indicating URLs that are not referring to the same domain as the destination URL.

Landing pages featuring fake close habits, pop-ups, overs or under.

Trapping mouse (i.e., back button disabled).

Ads requiring the submission of personal information (Social Security number, email, telephone number, etc.), except for e-commerce, where it has been made clear that a product is for sale.

Landing pages with Facebook references (though limited Facebook references in title body or image are allowed to clarify a destination).

Marks, logos, graphics, or product names on Facebook.

This implies Facebook endorses your product, services or advertising.

Features emulating Facebook.
Ads that do not contribute to the content of the landing page.

Ads that do not reflect the advertiser's business, product or brand.

Unfounded claims to quote the Facebook Ads terms of service, "including but not limited to costs, discounts or product availability."

Ads that endanger users.

Any ads "fake, deceptive, malicious or disappointing."
Ads that automatically play audio.

This one is a beauty: Ads will not be allowed in cases where a business model or practice is deemed unacceptable or contrary to the overall philosophy of Facebook advertising (whatever that means).

Ads that consumers complain about or that breach

"community standards." Swearing, obscenity, or "inappropriate language." "Obscene, defamatory, libelous, slanderous, and/or illegal content." Restricted goods, like tobacco products, explosives, firearms, paintball guns, BB guns, or weapons of any kind.

Ads that promote gambling, including online casinos, sports bets, bingo or poker, without Facebook authorization.

"Scams, illicit activity, or chain letters." Get-rich-quick schemes, work-from-home offers, full-time and part-time job alternatives, NSA money offers, or profit for no or small investment.

Ads for adults or dating sites that have sex as their subject.

Sex-toys ads, videos, or other products.

Ads for drugs that are not certified.

Ads on spy cams or other surveillance equipment. Non-accredited college diplomas web. "Religious inflammatory content." Terrorist agendas, or speech.

Commercial use of political items hot button, with or without a policy agenda.

"Hate speech, whether directed to an individual or a group, and whether based on the race, sex, religion, national origin, religious affiliation, marital status, sexual orientation, gender identity or the language of that individual or group."

Negative campaign ads.

The description of health conditions is derogatory or false.

Distributing to any third party data collected from campaigns.

Showing user data in advertisements, such as names or images of profiles.

Use of the data for any other reason than Facebook ads.

Personal targeting irrelevant; age, location, interest, and gender targeting must be important to the product.

Targeting adult themes to any consumer under the age of 18, "including abortion, sex education and health conditions."

Ads pointing to dating sites unless the relationship settings are set to "single." Must select a single value for male or female and target individuals over age 18, interest targeting parameter must be set to "single." Fraudulent offers.

Announcements that include a price, discount or "free" offer if the destination page is not the same as the offer and the same deal that the ad offers. The ad has to tell you what actions are required.

Subscription services do not meet strict restrictions. Whether you offer "ringtones, games, or other entertainment items, or any platform that causes a customer to sign up for a product or service's recurring billing," check FB Ads TOS. Ads for alcohol are also strictly limited in FB. It's very picky stuff from antisocial behavior, glorifying smoking or even ads glorifying the amount of alcohol by volume. If you are selling booze, go over to TOS Facebook Ads and review the rules.

Infringement of the rights of any third party, "including copyright, mark, privacy, advertising, or other personal or proprietary rights." Spam, as defined by laws, regulations, or industry norms. Incentives to click on ads or to give information about yourself.

Links in advertisements or landing pages that propagate downloads of spyware/malware including redirection.

Links in advertisements or landing pages which mine data from computers of users without consent.

Find usernames and passwords on Twitter.

For quick Facebook logins, proxy Facebook usernames and passwords.

Sneaky software which leads to unexpected user experience, including hidden downloads of different types.

Ads with bad grammar, incomplete sentences, repeated words (for example, "buy, buy, buy"), misspelled words, incorrect spacing, or schemes for capitalization.
Just capitalized acronyms.

Punctuation or exclamation points wrong or excessive.

Symbols in ads that do not correspond with the proper use of the symbol (for example, "$ave" instead of "save") or substitute entire terms (for example, "&" instead of "and" or" "$instead of "cash/dollars/money"), except where the symbol is part of the product or brand name.

A number of people have been suing famous Facebook Lawsuits on Facebook. We have been suing spammers and winning too.

Here are a couple of cases for and against broad F.

November 2008: Facebook v. Adam Guerbuez and Atlantis Blue Capital In 2008, Facebook received $873 million in damages for spamming users via personal Facebook messages against defendants Adam Guerbuez and Atlantis Blue Capital. This case was the highest record decision under CAN-SPAM. (The full name of the CAN-SPAM Act is Controlling the Assault of Non-Solicited Pornography and Marketing Act of 2003.) June 2009: Facebook v. Sanford Wallace In the case against Sanford Wallace, self-described "spam king," Facebook received $711 million in a court judgment. Wallace was charged with gaining access to Facebook accounts by fraudulent means and then using the accounts to conduct phishing scams.

February 2010: Nine Facebookers v. Facebook Nine Facebook users filed two class-action lawsuits resulting from misappropriated personal information in relation to the then-recent privacy settings revisions. Those filing the suits argued the settings were deceptive and contributed to the accidental sharing of personal data which was then leveraged for commercial use.

August 2010: Cohen and Orland v. Facebook Robin Cohen and Marcia J. Orland from the Los Angeles area are suing Facebook in response to the seemingly popular "Like" button that appears on the ads of the social network. Cohen and Orland say that their children, both under the age of 18, are being manipulated for profit-making purposes when they have already "liked" "like" advertising they see mutual friends. The parents argue that parental consent should be needed before Facebook.com leverages "like" data for commercial purposes.

October 2010: Facebook v. Spammers The social networking website filed three lawsuits in the U.S. federal court in San Jose, California, against persons allegedly trying to dupe Facebook members into registering for mobile spam subscriptions, thereby infringing its terms and applicable law. The defendants, Steven Richter, Jason Swan, and Max Bounty, Inc., are charged with running more than 27 fake profiles, 13 fake pages, and at least seven applications associated with an affiliate marketing advertising scam.

October 2010: Nancy Walther Graf v. Facebook Nancy Walther Graf of Minnesota sues game developer Zynga for allegedly selling personal information to Facebook users for money. The plaintiff alleges that the corporation has knowingly distributed personal data including the real names of customers to third-party advertisers and marketers without user consent, in breach of Zynga's arrangement with Facebook, Inc., and privacy laws. Walther Graf seeks U.S. class-action status. District court in the California Northern District.

The Facebook Ads Ethical Marketer's Rules of Engagement is

a prodigal channel, a tactical road for marketers to embark on a journey to attain carefully thought-out goals, perhaps in tandem with others. Take care when targeting users to get ad impressions to understand the audience you are communicating with and how your ads jive.

Because the advertisements are contextually targeted, advertisers ' acquiescence to users is more tacit than searching, where users ask for specific outcomes. The psychological structure is, therefore, a lot different. It is almost as if advertisers are welcomed to close-knit virtual communities where members of the community are linked by the nature of who they are rather than physical boundaries. Users press those little Xs that will make those advertising go down. If enough users take the trouble to indicate that they are annoyed by your ad, Facebook presumably bans the ad from showing. Here's what we think is the best practice when serving socially targeted advertisements.

Follow the law There is at least some form of intellectual property protection in almost every part of the world, including text, pictures, catchphrases, logos, product names, and other properties. At the end of the day, the single most important factor is adopting regulations for the jurisdiction in which marketing is conducted.

There have been a number of instances in the search

environment where litigants slugged out how laws are applied to activating advertisements with keywords, using trademarks or brand marks in ad copies, and using copyrighted materials. The definitions of slander and libel were litigated, adjudicated and challenged throughout the legal history, and lots of laws were made. Scams are scams, be they perpetrated on Twitter or in the back alley. Fraud is a fraud, error is negligence.

Such forms of cases are old news in traditional channels and the result. In fact, many companies have regulations governing where and how to make ads. In certain parts of the world, there are (or are not) certain restrictions on tobacco, booze, sex, drugs and gambling.

Gross and subtle distinctions between applicable laws would easily penetrate Facebook in itself in the United States, England, China, Australia and everywhere else in the world. There are however basic laws that will help keep you out of trouble if followed.

Note: I am not an attorney so do not consider this as legal advice. For advice on your specific situation please visit with your professional internationally trained law firm.

Don't say that you haven't violated the law yet, because your ad is still running. TOS breaches can get Facebook to kick you off.

Violating the law can well do away with your business and ruin your life.

Don't say something untrue. All kinds of assertions should be rooted in facts that are documented and indisputable. That said, telling the truth, again and again, does not prevent you from being sued. It can cost a crazy amount of money, especially when dealing with big companies to respond to even a frivolous action brought against you.

Read and understand the license for whatever artistic content you purchase. If you are working with an independent contractor to create intellectual property that can be used in your ads and landing pages, make sure that the contractor is clear of restrictions on intellectual property. The last thing any business needs is to be sued for ripping out the intellectual property of someone else.

Be on guard against highly aggressive marketing activities. If in doubt, do not. We can't find any case law specifying what's legal or not about activating Facebook Ads by targeting brand-name fans from other firms who have shared the brand's tenderness in their interests. It is reasonable to expect that there will be some case law in the near future since it is a major hot button. Remember and always clarify to clients and/or your employer that such actions will lead to legal exposure.

As modern as it is, ads on Facebook still amounts to gun slinging in the old Wild West. They are more than happy to sell you the ability to target people "like" Martha Stewart or Malt-O-Meal, irrespective of their future legality or where the data comes from on the social graph in terms of privacy settings.

Don't believe that you're not someone that you are. In some parts of the world running a sock, puppet avatar is literally against the law. The legal noose is beginning to close in on those in the US who post fake reviews. More US states pass laws that criminalize impersonation online.

Follow Service Words. When it comes to what we can and can not sell on Facebook, the constraints emerged largely from (a) the awful ads Facebook embraced when the site was small, and (b) the relentless affiliate marketers spamming the tar out of Facebook users. While most marketers fudge here and there a bit, it won't work for anyone to find sneaky ways to market restricted products such as lotteries or pharmaceutics.

Only things that have real value in the market. It's said the only real way to attain wealth is through value creation. The best campaign on Facebook Ads is for a product that is not sucking. In the marketing business, an age-old adage is that "you can't wrap up a turd in a pretty bow" and expect happy customers, good reviews and repeat business. Don't be in denial about "interest" and what a targeted user really means. Again, just don't do it if it feels wrong. If the test shows users don't care about it, stop. We saw a group reaction beginning with a single user's dedicated and vocal anxiety that eventually mushroomed into company credibility problems.

Ads on Facebook are a double edge sword. While we may reap the benefits of serving ads in an atmosphere in which users can easily share with their peeps something positive that they have found, disdain is just as easy to propagate. Trust me, one twisted Facebook user can be a source of stress, legal bills, and sales missed. Don't market such goods that have little or no interest. It could come back to bite you or your customer. Trust your instincts and don't fool yourself or anyone else.

Hold promises. Think of ad copying as promising, aligned with a landing page that keeps the promises. Strive to make landing pages validate the clicks of the users with an "Atta boy (or girl), way to click on the most suitable ad. You're in the perfect place now. "Don't be too crazy. Last February I was approached by an advertiser who was offering outpatient psychological services, targeting women between 50 and 60 in a very small rural Minnesota region. He wanted to target those involved in Alcoholics Anonymous with statements such as, "If Going to AA is Not Enough to Get Over Your Horrible Divorce," and "Being

Drunk Didn't Help, Going to AA Didn't Help" etc. We didn't get the job done. Coming from a recovery background, I knew the creep-factor with which I was comfortable transcended such messaging.

Facebook ads are both manipulative and beautiful. There is a deep psychological pull that appears to be taking place in closely focused populations. Our organization helps market a well-recognized series of online marketing conferences. The campaign was all about SEO, PPC, social media— all things that I personally love and share in my social graph. Our team has launched a number of ads that have ended up targeting my Facebook page. I clicked on those advertisements, again and again, only to find that my own shop's targeting prowess had taken me in! The targeting and ads are just that deep, resonating beyond visceral on a level. Please watch your step. Be gentle on that. Don't be excruciating in manipulating the feelings and perceptions of people.

Manipulate for service only. We are in the channel, on the other hand, to make money, friends or both. The trickery and ingenuity that lead users to a conclusion that serves mutual needs are completely in order. Reasonable exploitation could include commercials that end up being served to fans of a rival, say for a fresh, better, and cheaper product and without exposing the ad's competitive nature until the landing page.

Making chocolate lovers drool over a fantastic picture of truffles on the way to a landing page about a fabulous book of candy recipes is not wrong. Targeted at high school-age athletes and their parents, brand orthopedic surgery is not out of bounds. Check if the desired result of the ad and landing page actually represents the customer when it gets to clever-time.

We also question clients, "If that cat is rescued by the bionic fireman from the burning house, is the cat any less dead?"Of course, deception was taking place: the fireman wasn't actual, but the cat's not dead, right? Ergo, exploit for serving purposes only.

Set KPIs which are practical. We're going to get into this in much more detail later, but consider this for now: with their Facebook ad campaigns, many marketers are getting poor results. People came to us saying, "What is it that gives? We served 80 million impressions but only 0.02 percent of the CTR (click-through ratio). On average, the visitors stayed on the landing page for 50 seconds, drilled into the main site, but didn't buy it. "OK, let's look. First, for many Facebook Ads campaigns, .02 percent is a fine CTR. For that, Facebook will not be shutting down the commercial. Second, that's 80 million impressions, which brand the product to almost everybody who sees the ads. The other side of a CPC low CTR (cost per click) ad with a massive volume of impression is the incredibly low CPM (cost per thousand impressions). Google could cost more than five times the CPM. The campaign as an incredibly low-cost and highly targeted branding play may be justified. Had adequate expectations been set, the perception of success may have changed.

Sure, Facebook ads can be a great direct response, channels for first-touch sales. We all know however that many conversions require more than one customer interaction. Planning what the advertisements are for. Set goals that are practical. Don't worry.

CHAPTER THREE

Key Performance Indicators (KPIs)

There's a lot of ways of saying a goal. Goal, ambition, intent, purpose, hope, wish.   The term for goal, KPI, means key performance measures in marketing. I love that term when referring to marketing targets because the use of the word metric means that someone, somewhere, is actually planning to test something to show performance! Sounds simple but we know multinationals that don't set KPIs.

The marketing universe is full of absent, badly set and unrealistic KPIs. That's mind-blowing because the most KPI tracking technology has been in operation for years. On the other hand, identifying and monitoring conversions can be a lot of work–a major challenge, especially in the world of social media. This chapter deals with the definition of KPIs as applied to Facebook Ads.

Setting Expectations The channel can be extremely robust in the hands of savvy marketers because Facebook ads reach such a massive sampling of people, targeted with an incredibly personal focus. Conversely, the kiss of marketing death could be set out to use Facebook ads with unrealistic expectations about what can be achieved. I can't tell you how many industry peers I have come across since the 2007 release of the platform that acted like Facebook ads was a waste of time, money and effort. Its disdain is explained easily. They tried to use Facebook Ads to get the wrong KPIs.

I was fortunate because when I first rolled up my sleeves, I worked for a small audio recording-career college. Now that I understand Facebook's past and timing, I understand that the FB group has changed from including just college students to including high school students too. There were over 21,000 people in the United States still in early 2008 who liked "Las Vegas Vacation." Targeting capabilities blew my mind; they were evidently revolutionary. Instead of targeting "audio recording college, Minneapolis" searches, now the advertisement was to "single high school senior males" who wanted to "play guitar in a band" or "sing in a band." Setting attainable KPIs on Facebook has much to do with not putting undue pressure on promotions to perform beyond Facebook ads ' natural place in the marketing mix. Be aggressive: Make your marketing object a household name in the browsers of the right 30,600 people.

Check sales of direct response with impelling calls for action. A segment of fanatical gardeners living in New York City might just be susceptible to a reasonable sales pitch for an "organic garden in a barrel." By setting expectations for Facebook Ads, demographics match the intent of the ad.

Two hundred and eighty 60-plus-year-old men involved in prostate-online.com may not be eligible for mountain rescue team volunteer service. You get the picture.

Facebook will cost 10 to 50 percent less than Google's Display Network, based on cost per thousand impressions (CPM). I heard it said that "Facebook ads are kind of like what would happen if the Display Network worked really well." Don't equate the click-through ratio (CTR) of Facebook ads to the search; you're not going to be happy. Compare it to contextual products from Google and Bing, instead. Compare CTR to the assets shown in AOL or Yahoo!. Facebook is incinerating the competition in girth and a raw targeting could. Expect CTR from.15 percent up to 1.0 percent, with clicks costing between $.02 and up to $1.00. Expect prodigal length, and conversion may have been known to match or surpass hunt.

Manage the aspirations of your marketing team about the strengths and weaknesses of Facebook Ads. Challenging the thought of each. Ask, "Is this headline really going to mean something for our customers, as described by the demographic segment?"Manage the expectations of your boss by setting the role of Facebook in the Conversion Funnel. Check enough that the team is theoretically able to know the answer to the greatest extent possible.

Defining KPIs

The real value of Internet marketing is that it is technically easy to set up analytics by source, then roll them all up for insights needed to direct/redirect spending on marketing. Hence, it is important to set clear and discernible KPIs for marketing.

Executing marketing campaigns in any form is a strategy, perhaps one of many techniques that could include a marketing manager. Other tactics online and offline could include Google PPC, Bing SEO, newspaper ads, radio commercials, and small aircraft pulling long banner signs across Miami Beach during the spring break.

It's essential to understand that Facebook Ads are a medium where we're using strategies to sell stuff. Think of the ideal KPI as what we want to accomplish and channel strategies as the where and how we conduct campaigns to attain the KPIs.

Best practices involve explaining what we want to accomplish in plain language, committing to exact statistics and identifying a measurement system. Our shop specifies KPIs in writing, in advance and in plain language sentences at the project level. Here are some examples of KPI phrases. Notice that each state what we want to achieve and measure: sell 1,256 snarly widgets in a month, at an average cost of $17.75 per operation (CPA).

Get 65,000 video views at an average cost per view of $.08, and push 2.5 percent of viewers to access a white paper to a page on our company website.

Serve 50 million ad impressions over two weeks, for an average cost of $.43 and 6 percent conversion to a product purchase on the landing page.

Allow 22,000 new fans for us to connect with our company page and comment on later.

Mine 345,000 email addresses for women under the age of 27 from Canada, the United States, the United Kingdom, and Australia.

Serve 200 million branding impressions, so that the oil spill in the Gulf does not spook our stockholders.

Note that the KPIs example doesn't address how we're going to get things done, only what we want to get done and what metrics indicate success. There is nothing on what the advertisements are going to say or what the landing page is going to be. Working with stakeholders is the role of the account manager to determine what needs to be done, and how to measure success— the KPIs. It is then the task of the channel tactician to figure out how to best attain the KPIs and what channels to use.

Popular KPIs haven't changed much during the evolution of marketing channels. We advertisers are still doing pretty much what marketers do. We sell stuff. We're branding things. We set out to achieve targets using channel strategies and appealing to human nature by somehow swaying attitudes or engaging audiences at some scalable point in some way. Do not get replaced by new paradigms such as mobile applications or other digital products. A selling is yet a sale. Branding remains a brand. Although goods and methods of distribution have evolved and new product groups exist, the main marketing activities have not really changed much at all.

This is a fortunate fact, particularly for old people like me, because almost everything I learned about tactical marketing before the Internet was applied to new models in Germany. Therefore, when we determine the rightful place of Facebook Ads in any marketing mix, it's a helpful exercise to note the "modern" mix of KPIs.

KPIs have historically been distributed across a subset of old-school disciplines and separated loosely by marketing, advertisement, and public relations. Let's look at key performance metrics from the viewpoint of a classic marketer, and understand how Facebook ads will work when implemented.

Note, every KPI will state specifically what the target is, and how it will be calculated. Channel strategies of some KPIs do measure ad performance in terms of cost per click (CPC), cost per action (CPA), click-through ratio (CTR), cost per thousand impressions (CPM), or impression count. That said, precise estimation is sometimes not possible in advance, but in many cases, we are willing to give approximate figures. You should always presume that running test ads are a requirement for deciding the ongoing budget, at the outset of any campaign. If that is the case, say so in the KPI statement channel tactics section. We concentrated on the inclusion in the first examples of campaign ad performance metrics and later on innovation. We make sure that we state the budget in later instances.

Each of the example KPIs would also be implemented in conjunction with other networks in all probabilities. We are focusing solely on the Facebook Ads component of the marketing mix for the purpose of this chapter.

Branding KPIs: Seeding Tomorrow's Conversions Today
Branding is when the KPI is not simply concerned with making
an immediate transaction, with full understanding that many
transactions require multiple encounters with a company to
close. Here are a few examples and the methods of correlating
Facebook Ads to help you achieve the KPIs.

KPI Raising awareness among Europeans about our fashion
eyewear, as calculated by Google's Insights for Search Tool for our
brand term keyword.

Facebook ads channel strategies Five hundred million global
impressions in a three-day rotation at $.24 CPM throughout the
year, showcasing our positioning message, logo and stunning
customers wearing our glasses.

KPI Lift Google AdWords direct response search sales for our
luxury hotel in Chicago as measured by CTR and associated
quality score after making our brand a household name for people
who love Chicago and do not live in two Illinois states.

Facebook Ads channel tactic Sixty million impressions at $.21
CPM, in rotation and at a.06 percent Facebook CTR, showing
images of iconic Chicago festivals, four to six weeks before, in the
same marketplaces we serve. Amplify AdWords direct festival
name response search PPC, offering discounts to festival

attendees staying at our hotel.

The time to sell her national practice and hospital affiliations to an orthopedic surgeon is not when the squad of high school soccer captain blows his knee out. In this case, branding could mean Facebook ads offering to share the results of a new study on athletes ' nutrition and avoid injury. Aim the campaign for football players of high school age and their guardians. For a fact, the good doctor could be offering free wellness services year after year for varsity players, mom, and dad. Naturally, when little Willem wrecks his knee at the tournament of the state championship, his mom and dad are more likely to ask the orthopedic doctor who has become a trusted adviser. Such is what branding is all about.

Branding can also be an opportunistic practice, in a kind of reverse crisis management. If your restaurant receives a glowing review in the Sunday Times, a plugged-in blogger raves about your new product, or you make the Inc. 500, in an opportunistic response, these are great times for the brand.

Today's branding is the transfer of tomorrow. Facebook ads are super-cool for branding, as they concentrate on the deep-seated desires of consumers. The regional branding concept, which is extremely cheap, has already become the new wave of local marketing in the hands of smart marketers. The same is true for a truly massive global scale of foreign marketplaces. Branding is a classic marketing target for KPIs and Facebook Ads can be a gigantic channel strategy for achieving KPI branding.

KPIs with Direct Response: Need Conversion Now?

Direct response (DR) means calling users to act now, to get a conversion operation to completion. Although often used to denote an immediate sale, DR can mean any desired result of the transfer, including lead generation, event signups, free download of applications and many other actions. The limiting factor in making a pitch direct response is the intention of the marketer to close the deal now. By nature, advertisements tend to be more aggressive, sponsoring benefits such as price, quality, service and limited-time offers.

Facebook ads can work well for DR conversions, but as a general thumb rule, a DR conversion channel isn't as good as search. There are exceptions, however. For years, we've been attracting Facebook users interested in "apprentice electrician," between the ages of 35 to 45, to sign up for free Yellow Pages – type products with advertisements that read, "Market Your Electrician Contractor Business Online For Free." We've had success selling concert tickets to aficionados of specific artists as well as with college and university lead generation, sale of beauty products, mobile apps, and many other "convert 'em now" sales plays. We've hawked $2.oo-off vouchers for sugary breakfast cereal to pot smokers and converted like gangbusters. Here are some fantastic DR KPI examples: Facebook Ads channel strategy Ten million views, in rotation and at a.03 percent Facebook CTR, showing pictures of oil-spill-tainted birds and urban blight targeted to employees of government environmental protection agencies and users involved in agriculture, recycling, conservation, the world's rainforests, and other related interests. Market to the Facebook application page directly after using FB's internal "Connections" metric for segmentation of conversions. Establish, assess, and maintain costs.

KPI Extend our international English-speaking customer base into Canada, the Us, Australia, New Zealand, Spain, and Portugal through new monthly shipments of 350 medium-duty treadmills over and above units currently sold in these countries combined.

Facebook Advertising channel strategy In a two-per-weekday rotation, check hard-core call-to-action advertising rotating offers of free international shipping, weekly specials, celebrity endorsements, and other genuinely useful inducements to buy now. Estimates are $9,500.

So, while some are going to tell you that Facebook Ads is a terribly weak DR channel, make up your own mind with clever targeting and calls to action. Just take advantage of your head.

DR conversion that surrounds digital media such as video plays in YouTube or free white papers tends to be easy because the user requires little commitment. There are plenty of dancing ninja marketers, however, who are experts at separating consumers from their hard-earned cash with a tap of one landing page. Such is the direct-response marketer's Zen.

Friendly KPIs: One Is Silver and the Other's Gold Because Facebook is a place about friendship, it's natural to set up KPIs about making new friends. Sharp-shooting advertisers nowadays are producing reports showing cost-per-friend and cost-per-click Facebook ads and a new count of fans.

This trend has become super-competitive, as fanged advertisers target each other's followers, including open warfare. There has been litigation and case law in the search space, but as of this writing, the concept of targeting brand-themed friends of others by targeting Precise Interests has yet to be fully defined lawfully. Expect the evolution of American and international law in terms of this method of targeting. That being said, few might doubt the value of targeting people who love to cook organic food, inviting them to friend the community of our recipe-and-wine-pairing blog.

Facebook apps can also be regarded as a' friendly' channel. Try describing friends as someone who accepts your generous offer to give friends special tools. Make the CAD drawings currently available in a list of 7,690 files with filename numbers available through a tag search through a Facebook application "search, select, preview, and download." Trust me, it'll be easy to get the CAD-file consumer to become your friend with a service application such as this. Here are some KPI friends on Facebook.

KPI Get 15,000 members of our Facebook community engaged by our competitors who want to like our Facebook page. Take advantage of the metric "Connections" and proper campaign segmentation to know data-certain that new fans from competitive segments are completely mined.

Facebook marketing strategies platform Target Facebook users interested in the top six brand words of our closest competitors like specific products. Rotate with a CTR of 0.02 percent two million observations, set costs, assess and retain costs. Push direct traffic to our Facebook page. Check ads that show our brand in the ads versus "blank" advertising (that means users figure out who our brand is after landing on the fan page).

Facebook ads channel strategy target Facebook users who are specifically involved in President Carter and others who are engaged in politics. Serve ads that extract potentially inflammatory or endearing quotes from the interview, which can shed light on different political factions of assorted persuasions and compel them to read more. Display Carter's pictures in both positive and subtly negative visual light to reinforce their prejudice and motivation the press, as necessary for the targeted section. The budget, one-time, is $12,500.

Facebook is a Past and Future Friends group. Using Facebook ads to get to know like-minded people just makes sense. Measure the approach, and take a slight step. Make sure your paid friendship overtures provide genuine value so the friendship will last as long as possible and help both users and your company.

Customer Service KPIs: The Holy Grail To many, the ideal convergence of trade and viral potential is the simple goal of enhancing customer service through social media platforms. There's a very little more effective response to user needs than immediate and publicly available response. What's cool about Facebook ads is that by targeting the users interested in the supported goods, they can be used to drive traffic to any customer support site. Drive customers to support pages, ranging from lists of phone numbers to YouTube video FAQs and/or support specialists in the live Twitter community manager. Using ads served in viral environments with destination URLs in other social media environments can be a beautiful thing to see and appreciate because the success is public, for all. Check out the KPIs from this case study.

KPI Increase the the use of Twitter's customer support platform for our industry-standard large-brand professional software suite for image editing. Measure an increase of 6 percent in followers, in / outbound tweets per day, and a reduction of.5 percent in traditional telephone support as measured by the volume of call centers, month over month for a quarter.

Facebook Advertising Tactic Network Target Facebook users under 28 who are interested in permutations of the brand terms of our product suite along with college students studying graphic design and digital photography and their professors who are most likely using our software. The ads promise faster response time, personalized attention and a more personal relationship with technical assistance. The landing page is a Twitter profile aid through a measurable redirect script. The budget is around $55,000 a month.

KPI Increase the use of our YouTube videos to serve clients with special dietary needs for low-sodium diets.

Facebook advertising channel strategies Especially target people interested in health problems that include bloating, water retention, healthy eating, heart health and low-sodium diets. Provide messages of hope and health, and connect to free video content.

Unfortunately, poor performance can amplify a bad experience in responding to clients in public and make you look pretty bad. Session organizers used Twitter really well during PubCon 2010 in Las Vegas, a legendary and cherished online marketing conference, to manage detailed inquiries and communicate with attendees. As is increasingly popular throughout the convention center, the conference showed the live Tweet stream on large monitors. Lunch supplies went down in flames on day one— a total disaster. There it was, front and center, page after page of horrific comments tweeted at the end of their ropes by hungry users.

Now, consumers are sure to hang out on Twitter, whether they're happy or pissed off. You can easily guide them and tell them where to get help. Facebook Advertising is an amazing platform for getting the message out on all the ways you serve clients.

Crisis management KPIs Classic crisis management is in some sense a stressful permutation of reverse branding to prevent damage control. The amazing specificity of Facebook Ads targeting can be a fast track right to the heart of reputation risk territory. Speak directly to those who may be affected, such as app users, business employees, doctors, psychologists or nuclear engineers. Pick out young parents concerned about baby food that has just been remembered. Below are some examples of positive KPIs and related Facebook platform tactics.

KPI Ensure that the whole community has the latest safety details from train derailment involving our chemical spill. Success will be assessed by driving 1,500 return visitors to our blog every hour for the duration of the crisis, who spend more than 45 seconds on the website before departure.

Facebook Advertising channel tactic Show ads, targeted to those within 10 miles of the spill, in the following sequence: announce the information service with headlines like "Worried about the chemical spill? Get important information here." If there's a new update, post ads that take care of the update.

Once the crisis is over, let the danger pass by to the citizens.
The budget is flexible, depending on the interest, duration of the crisis, etc.
KPI Offset negative publicity received at our 1,500-person workforce from several high-profile sexual harassment claims. Basically, this example is a permutation of KPI branding. Measuring KPIs by branding can be a tricky deal. In this scenario, we will begin to measure success by counting impressions aimed at potentially interested parties. The first phase of branding KPIs is a perception-that is, how often the ad is advertised. First, we'd home in on the click-through ratio, as an indicator of how well our message resonates with the target market. From there,

interaction metrics, as in time on page and page views per session, could be an indicator of meeting goals— especially if the landing page herds users towards an action, such as requesting more details, making a phone call, or signing up for SMS notifications.

Facebook ads channel tactic Run advertisements celebrating our pride in contributing to community low unemployment. Feature testimonials from individual employees about how to work for us is awesome and has changed their lives. Drag visitors to landing pages highlighting these individual employees, and information about our company's contribution to the local economy.

Using Facebook Ads, target those who may be affected when a crisis hits That's an amazing' in' for providing information, settling feelings, and otherwise engaging with customers that you know are crisis stakeholders. Keep in mind that app resistance isn't unheard of, so make sure to take a high road.

Don't gush, candy-coat, spin, or else attempt to massage results to be anything but real. Stake out a modest place, function to love honestly, and there is a great chance that things will work better. Keep in mind that common axioms still apply in public relations. Not all crises call for a response. Nevertheless, reaching for Facebook Ads will make a difference to the outcome when a public response is called up.

Community relations KPIs Community relations are all about how people perceive the place where you live your business. There are multiple congregations to work with companies with multiple locations. On the other end of things, coping with roadblocks from zoning ordinances to disgruntled residents outside the main gate can mean a poor relationship with the neighborhood. It's clear that supporting investment in the' hood can pay dividends and help avoid misunderstandings or even acrimony.

Almost every city, large or small, has civic organizations such as Rotary, the Salvation Army, the Junior League, Pop Warner Football, and high school soccer. Everywhere people live in even small concentrations there are a number of local issues. There are programs feeding the less fortunate, volunteer advocates, pet shelters and fund drives from United Way. In most cases, establishing critical partnerships at home represents a strong focus for companies.

Giving unconditional and good old-fashioned contact is the best way to keep things cool on the home front in terms of traditional public relations practices. Facebook ads for both can be a strong source. In Duluth, where I live, we volunteer a couple of times a year to talk in the marketing department at the University of Minnesota and take pride in regional economic growth. Until we speak, in the system we buy Facebook ads aimed at students and teachers that we think would be interested in. The St. Paul office at our company doubles as an art gallery and displays amazing paintings by up-and-coming local artists. What answer is, we don't know. Just the right thing to do is to help neighbors.

Serve friendly ads that raise awareness for the Kids Voting program, recruit volunteers to clean the beach, raise funds for breast cancer prevention, honor a respected outgoing university chancellor, welcome the UMD Bulldogs NCAA Division 1 women's national hockey champions or advertise a matching grant for public radio. Of the biggest rewards of my work are tasks like this.

KPI Increase our participation and exposure in our hometown through holistic engagement at the local grassroots level. Success will be measured by getting 500 RSVPs and 300 physical attendance at our annual United Way Chili Cook-off charity event on Facebook.

Facebook Ads channel tactic Organize this year's annual event using Facebook Events. Use the Facebook Events engine to send out 2000 invitations. To codify the invitation using Facebook Ads. The copy will read, "Do you still have an RSVP invitation to your Annual Chili Cook-off?"And push RSVP users. Offer free topping of cheddar-cheese to use Facebook for RSVP.

KPI Increase flood-relief donations by $23,000 in May for Grand Forks, North Dakota, by appealing to regional users who have shown a tendency to support such campaigns. Mobilize a 50-person volunteer team to fill four half trucks with donated bottled water and go to Grand Forks to distribute.

Facebook Advertising Network Tactics

A call to the community's sense of family by serving ads that draw attention to the tragedy of families losing their homes, senior citizens at risk, and health issues. Offer the solutions and help you get involved. Target people between college-age and age 30 who show interest in the Peace Corps, Salvation Army, Good Will, Red Cross, United Way and other charities. The onetime budget is $9,000.

Advertising has a definite place in relation to the community. Facebook Ads rocks the building since targeting individuals who are fanatically enthusiastic about pretty much anything is so easy. Earlier in this book, we're going to look at targeted sentiment among charities.

Internal Relations KPIs Internal relationships can be delicate, meaning those involving employees, vendors, board members and other stakeholders inside. Public relations experts will tell you a lot of businesses are failing to sell and advertise for themselves. Counsel also told us that contacting Facebook can be a sticky wicket. For example, we have the ability to easily target regional Facebook users who work with a self-reported affinity for a specific union at a particular company. Internal relations, especially in the age of social media, also have a cool everyday side to it.

Once again, an advertisement can have its location, provided the attribute targeting Facebook's education and workforce. Even where Facebook does not officially recognize smaller firms as targeted employers, employees often self-identify their workplace; Facebook's targeted occupation is often overlooked and extremely powerful. It's enough to say the workers are on Facebook, they can be contacted online, and it should be a smart path to pursue.

Promote an employee every month as an example to the entire staff, advertise on snowy days to remind the team of parking outside the plant, or thank everyone for their exceptional work during the merger. Host a corporate baby-cute contest or recruit staff at the homeless shelter for volunteer work. A valuable human resources tool could be the ability to target your own employees with Facebook Ads.

KPI Leverage the personal relationships of employees and turn 200 of those friends and family into brand ambassadors who patronize our restaurant deli. Success will be calculated by a redemption rate of 45 percent on our free meal voucher for friends and family.

Facebook Ads channel Friends-and-Family tactic coupon for free Ruben or Rachael sandwich "in gratitude for our employees and their families" and in exchange for our Facebook deli page. The landing page promises a continuing program of discounts for friends and family in the future. The budget amounts to $6,600 a month.

KPI Employees reassure that cutbacks in seven cities are not destabilizing the business and things are still going strong.

Facebook Advertising Strategies channel

Target our own workers, with special emphasis on employers and their officers. To evaluate ad copy and to navigate the delicate balance concerning these sensitive issues, please consult with our public relations firm and lawyer. The budget is as demand dictates, $4,000 or less.

Public relations ads can be as plain as revealing the annual picnic venue or as subtle as a company-wide inculcation of gratitude for a job well done and a deal accomplished. Find Facebook's efficacy as a conduit as compared with more traditional means such as lunchroom posters, fax, business cafeteria table tents, and endless meetings. To start with, Facebook's message delivery to internal stakeholders is observable, so that we can determine how many times the ad was viewed, which groups of audiences saw and clicked on the advertisement and activity on the landing page. When working with workers is sometimes a Rubik's Cube, an arrow in the quiver is certainly immediate access to your team with targeted Facebook adverts.

Investor Relations

KPIs Almost every company has a certain financial goal. Customers and creditors are searching for signs as to the solvency of any company. Facebook ads can be easily targeted at members of the city council weighing potential government contract awards or bankers considering a loan to finance your next growth phase. Angel investors are particularly fertile ground for branding in finance. Does that sound foolish? I think that sounds very imaginative.

For a second, do not doubt that serving subtle messages to existing investors can instill confidence and inspire patience, as things grow slightly slower than expected. Don't discount the possibility of using your branding messages to move an angel investor over the course of months. Although in America there are significant laws and regulations covering even the appearance of impropriety in manipulating stock prices, corporations are certainly allowed to market, promote their goods, and manipulate things the way they want to. Let's be no Pollyanna. Serving ads can be a terrific business for your financial stakeholders!

Although discretion is typically wise, it is meritorious in some cases to show the face of public finance. The announcement of major contracts, the introduction of a new executive recruit and the demand for a fabulously successful product launch or the grand opening of a new factory will instill trust between creditors and investors.

KPI Soften the pre-IPO marketplace to create more buzz around the upcoming process for our new market-defining smartphone product. Since we're going to target journalists and feed them messages setting out the revolutionary strengths of the product, we're going to measure this KPI through blog posts, trade pub buzz and major media mentions.

Note: Look for the intersection of investor relationships and media relationships by targeting branding messages to financial writers for influential publications that cover the market place.

Facebook ads channel tactic Feature ads to stock market stakeholders, bankers, entrepreneurs, stockbrokers, and those working for wealth management companies. Announce new goods, recent achievements, and awards received, and thank union members for the latest three-year work contract that is mutually supportive and welcoming. The budget for four months preceding the IPO announcement is not to exceed $35,000 per month.

KPI Use social media to boost the distribution of the national electricity utility annual report to 8,600 (an increase of 20 percent). Reduce the cost of printing and paper in the second year. Attain paperless delivery within 4 years. Nurture the impression of the world that our firm is green and environmentally responsible.

Facebook ads channel tactic Ads offers free download of the annual report to anyone. Aim the advertising to those who should be interested but typically are not part of the distribution. That includes politicians, professors of economics and large-scale industry captains.

Speak to an attorney first if you have any questions about marketplace advertising's legality with the goal of shaping the public perception of financials.

Media Relations KPIs When you are loved by respected

reporters, bloggers, TV journalists, publishers and radio disc jockeys, the whole world often follows. It is also true that reporters dislike your company when it is not good. Clearly, establishing partnerships with media types that are mutually nourishing will pay wonderful dividends. Because Facebook ads are targeting a matrix of workplaces and interests of users, the best marketers are delivering carefully crafted messages that target journalists squarely.

Remember however, there are over 500 million users on Facebook. It is easy to market to 300 journalists, or even a few, who work for a single newspaper. To believe that great Facebook marketers would choose not to take advantage of this amazing opportunity to delicately influence the most powerful influencers would be naive.

KPI Back up a Minnesota Twins baseball player's attempt to get into the Hall of Fame. Influence major baseball writers who vote for which players to earn the award each year.

Facebook ads funnel strategy Target those who work for AP, Gannett, McClatchy, USA Today, ESPN, TV stations in every market, and individual newspapers in every market, and who are involved in "sports writing," "football writers," and prominent current and past baseball players. Focus on messages thanking fans for years of support and lobbying for the new Minneapolis baseball stadium. For three months the budget is $7,000 a month.

KPI A lawmaker is targeting prominent bloggers, radio jocks and local morning show hosts to elicit demands for interviews.

Facebook Advertising channel strategies Aim using the bucket of work and education, clearly targeting the very media workers we want to respond to. Test progress by demanding interviews via phone calls and type submissions.

When a strong blogger asks us for an interview or feature story, we like to think, "Oh, he's got us right where we want him." Little does our new friend realize we worked his impression of our business for months, shaping his knowledge slowly and subtly. It is important to say that media-oriented marketing messages cannot be a bunch of junk or free. Marketers know you cannot wrap a turd in a bow and expect the smell to be enjoyed by customers. Likewise, tread lightly when selling to the media, and don't hold a stick at all.

Research and Message-Testing KPIs We used to test marketing messages in focus groups in the olden days. Herding a supposedly representative cross-section of our customers into a hotel room was popular, feeding them croissants and gaging their reactions to our beta campaign themes. Digital marketing has revolutionized the technique of message-testing and transformed the process into an exciting math problem.

Multivariate message research was first conducted by search marketers in the mid to late 1990s and is the standard in technical advertising. Marketers rotate dozens, hundreds, or even thousands of headlines and body copy permutations on a regular basis to prove which magic combination solves the sales puzzle.

Long gone are the days of basing major campaigns on a small sampling of opinion. Now we're deciding which messages function in the vast crucible of serving our most significant audiences with hundreds of millions of impressions aimed head-on. Each of the ad platforms of the major search engines has some kind of built-in algorithm-driven tool for multivariate message testing.

KPI Prove which positioning message for public relations is more convincing for our "ordinary" mobile phone customer as demonstrated by their ability to force clicks. We are searching for messages that for non-sales messaging result in more than 8 percent CTR on a consistent basis.

Facebook ads tactics channel Rotate to four messaging statements and logo concepts delivered from our PR company. Serve a different designated market area (DMA) for each cluster: New York, Los Angeles, St. Louis, and Minneapolis. Check each logo design combined with each of the four marketing messages we're testing to show the best combination of logo and message. Target all those who live in the DMA and are older than 20. Expect relatively low CTR because the ads do not contain any value state, only the positioning statement. We are looking for individually compelling statements. The budget is $30,000 for one month per marketplace, for a total of $120,000.

KPI Prove which audiences in the launch process should buy a new product, and in answer to which news and picture concepts.

Facebook Ads channel strategies Build bracketed messages and photos for research, ensuring a wide range of different concepts are tested out. For each social group, display the advertisements in insular geographic areas to avoid pollution of the messages. Measure CTR for the combinations and sales of different headline segments.

In most cases, when an advertiser gives us headlines and body copy to use for advertisements, the first questions we ask are, "Why are you sure this method of copying works?"Then," Why did you prove it?"We have not done so many times, or the longitudinal study is dubious because a sample is too small. Why attribute decisions such as this to subjective inference when there is absolute data?

Do you want to sell tons of detergent that extracts oil and

gasoline from working clothes? Check planned to message to proprietors of 211,000 car mechanics, foremen and laundromat. Sell sporty high-end bags? Target test ads for college hockey players, managers of team equipment, used sports goods shoppers and people who love going to NFL games. Do you market the new iPhone app on a hot recipe website that mashes the cooking experience of in-store food? Check those commercials that are whipping up Baked Alaska and glazed duck.

It's clearly irresponsible not to take advantage of the hyperactive personal modeling offered by Facebook to learn what works: what to say and to whom.

Facebook Ads and Attribution

Most conversion tracking to this point in the online marketing context has been "the last touch," meaning a user visits before the transaction, lead, or other target occurred as calculated from the last page. By instinct, we have always known that many KPIs require multiple visits before users buy, but most marketers have no analytics technology to prove it. The industry standard is now changing to calculate conversions through attribution models, where we analyze multiple visit series, touched pages, and so on. Time after time, we see Facebook ads proving to be "introductory" first-touch ads, which encourage repeat visits and ultimately lead to sales.

There are currently a few management tools for Facebook Ads that support turnkey attribution. Acquisio, Omniture, Marin Software, and ClickEquations are the first tools to bundle attribution into their product management platform ads. These tools are very expensive for bigger advertisers and only feasible. Facebook has been cautious in improving its application programming interface (API) and granting toolmakers access. We plan to develop more resources for attribution over time and to be released to the public.

Since Facebook grants bulk uploading and downloading of CSV (spreadsheet) to bigger advertisers, some marketers have built custom applications centered on spreadsheet logic engines. Though pretty clunky these spreadsheet apps can be very successful.

It takes neither a custom application nor a fancy algorithm to think through this conundrum. Facebook users are the same people who use Google and Bing to search for. There are so many users on Facebook that common sense dictates they overlap. Going a step further, it is reasonable to assume that before searching, the users who search may be affected. No doubt Facebook is a place to do just that. While attribution analytics as of this writing is not affordable to most marketers, confident marketers understand that Facebook ads can play a role early in a multi-touch conversion process, which is potentially crucial for the ultimate conversion.

CHAPTER FOUR

Designing your Ads

Web UI and Power Editor Two native user interfaces for ad creation and editing are available on Facebook. The Web UI is available on Facebook.com / advertising by the green "Create an Ad" button. The second access point is the "Power Editor" of FB. As of this writing, Power Editor has not been rolled out in any FB Ads account and is only open to FB Ads Members ' accounts. We provide Power Editor references as we expect that in the near future it will have a broader distribution because it solves a few important problems. You will find a link on the left-hand sidebar if you have access to the Power Editor.

Since the Facebook Ads Web UI is completely featured for Ad Creation and not the Power Editor, this chapter will review the ad creation screen for Web UIs. In any case, the Power Editor is essentially similar to the Web UI in the way FB Ads attributes are set up and exactly the same as the execution within each attribute.

The big difference is that for each main bank of attributes the Power Editor has separate screens, whereas the Web UI puts all of them on one page. It's facile to think about.

Module 1: Design Your Ad The first step in designing your ad is to select the destination — basically, the specific web page or Facebook page where users end up after clicking on the ad or sponsored story. The destination is generally termed a landing page. The first choice is to use an external URL, meaning any web page that is not Facebook's. In the Ad creation interface Design Your Ad module If you are a group, event, app, or page administrator, you have the option of linking directly to the assets you control over Facebook. Every advertisement qualifying will appear in the drop-down menu after you choose the option "I want to advertise something that I have on Facebook" from the drop-down menu Destination. Choosing to support a website or event provides marketers with options for including interactive features, such as Website buttons and event RSVPs.

Besides using Facebook Ads, you can also support stories about your brand that have organically bubbled up (surfaced) in the Facebook news feed (a result of users engaging with them). Sponsored stories aren't the same as ads and they are awesome; including them in your FB campaign naturally and inherently virally amplifies the actions of your target audience. Surfaceable stories include page likes, blog views, page post comments, check-ins, user shares, apps used, and played games, and domain tales.

The next step is to write a thrilling 25-character headline and somebody copy (up to 135 characters can be used). Complete the process of creating an ad by uploading an image to your ad, in GIF, JPEG or PNG format. Choose an image that is clearly visible when small because the maximum size for FB ad images is 110 or 80 pixels. Facebook can reduce the size of larger images but they may be distorted in ways you might not like unless they are proportionally right. My recommendation is to submit the picture at the right size so no surprises. Later we will explore the entire process of ad creation in more detail, The Suggest An Ad button* is available for an external URL and offers automatic ad creation. If available, the HTML title tag on the destination page will become the headline, and the meta description will be used as the body copy. Unless the owner of the external web page has chosen an image to use for FB (meta property="og: image), "the images posted on the destination page can be toggled. Automated ad production is practically useless most of the time unless the external destination URL is to a website that is set up very well.

A more recent alternative that can save quite a bit of time is the Select Existing Creative feature. Choosing this option opens a pop-up window, which lists each ad in the account. Choose an ad that would make a good starting point, and click Send. All creative elements of the original ad, including title, body copy and picture, will automatically fill the same attributes for the ad you are composing at the moment. What's cool is that as a starting point to mine completed ads to clone you can reach into any campaign in the account you're working on, including the ones deleted.

CHAPTER FIVE

Facebook's Powerful Targeting

The subsequent stage in the wake of designing your advertisement is to characterize social sections that determine which Facebook users will see it. The capacities are marvelous, a progressive distinct advantage.

Estimated Reach

Every one of the three main modules is comprised of different parameters, seeming through and through inside every module. This part gives a complete manual for the mechanics of the subsequent module in Facebook's promotion building UI: Targeting.

Probably the coolest thing about the UI is the Estimated Reach box, a dark square shape that drifts to one side of the Targeting module. Scroll up on the page and the Estimated Reach box stays moored to the highest point of the targeting module. Scroll down further into the targeting module's parameters and the box drifts down the page, consistently in view while targeting. Reach in age 18 and up in the United States—each of the 155, 771,580 of them as of this composition. The absolute props up and up.

Note: Remember, in spite of the fact that Facebook gives estimated to reach to paid advertisement targeting purposes, keen network supervisors explore Facebook's relative client socioeconomics for the accompanying reasons:

- To characterize networks in which to partake
- To increase a superior understanding with respect to relative sizes of said networks
- To contemplate contenders' devotees
- To finding new market fragments
- To reveal social portions that may mean different channels, for example, Twitter, YouTube, and search

The UI's Estimated Reach box, counting client include forecasts progressively, is an unfathomable segment inquire about apparatus unto itself. Ostensibly, this UI changed the promoting scene perpetually in light of the fact that it illuminates which users on Facebook are keen on what. Changes—even from minute to minute or program invigorate to revive—are not out of the ordinary, particularly as mixes of parameters become progressively mind-boggling. Additionally, the Web UI can be somewhat flaky, which is sensible for innovation, for example, this, served in an internet browser. Whenever Estimated Reach quits refreshing, simply invigorate the whole program window. More often than not, your work to that point will be lost, so take a screen catch of your advancement so you can rapidly type in any targeting thoughts you've lost. Another choice when the UI quits refreshing is to click, "Survey Ad," head to the following screen, and afterward click, "Alter Ad" to come back to the past screen. You ought not to lose any work.

Targeting Attributes

Advertisers finger Facebook users by picking esteems on a framework of attributes in the Targeting module of the promotion creation UI. Here is a text-tree diagram of main sections and attributes. Make a duplicate of this text-tree to use as a worksheet for preproduction arranging and other destroying sessions. We'll go into every one of them in detail, from an advertiser's point of view.

Area
- Nation (attribute)
- State/region (attribute)
- City (attribute)
- Urban communities inside ___ miles sweep (attribute)

Socioeconomics

- Age (attribute)
- Sex (attribute)

Interests (main section) Defaults to, "Exact Interests," Toggle to/from, "General Category Targeting"

- Associations on Facebook (unmistakable if goal is inner FB page)
- Users who are connected to (attribute)
- Users who are not effectively connected to (attribute)
- Users whose companions are connected to (attribute)
- Propelled Demographics (main section)
- Birthday (attribute)
- Sexual intrigue (attribute)
- Relationship status (attribute)
- Dialects (attribute)
- Instruction and Work (main section)
- College graduate (attribute)
- College (attribute)
- Major (attribute)
- In college (attribute)
- College (attribute)
- Major (attribute)
- Graduation years (attribute)
- In secondary school (attribute)

- Workplaces (attribute)

And Operator

The main focus sections— Location, Demographics, Interests, Facebook Connections, Advanced Demographics, and Education & Work — really work in a matrix. It implies that the selected values between each of these parts are between the operator and the selected values. In other words, Country selection: Brazil, Age: 22, and Interest: Baking means that the targeted users live in Brazil and are 22 years old and are also involved in baking.

Obviously specifying additional targeting attributes with the and operator reduces estimated to reach as the process filters down to users who display an exact combination of those attributes. It does make sense. Adding additional requirements using and emphasizing selection, as fewer Facebook users are more specifically addressed. In the UI there is no way to select the and the operator. Facebook makes those decisions and defincs them as hard presets. Here's an example: There are 141,221,000 people living in the United States (Facebook users) who are 18 years of age or older.

- There are 61,655,720 people living in the United States and being 18 years of age or older. Note that estimated reach has been reduced due to the filtering out of women.

- There are 565,020 people living in the United States who are 18 years of age or older and like NASCAR. Once, projected coverage is that because users not involved in NASCAR are filtered out now.

Many attributes use the and operator within the main sections. Choosing College Grad, for example, by itself filters users down to college graduates. Major and College are available as options when choosing to grade in college or college. Choosing College Grad, and then identifying College: Harvard and Degree: Biochemistry only promotes advertisements for Facebook users who have graduated from college and have gone to Harvard and have a Biochemistry Major.

Don't let this sneer at you. Just remember that with every new targeting attribute separated by the and the operator, the estimated reach is reduced. Later in this chapter, when we analyze each targeting attribute, we will take note of which values are influenced by preset and operators.

Or Operator

Some main section's attributes have the operator or the operator in between. Adding targeting criteria connected by target width, or increases it. The Bucket of Interests is a great example. Specific interests are concatenated with the or user within the bucket of Interest. Stipulating additional interests between increases in estimated reach with the or operator because we are adding more users that fit the targeting criteria. Which makes sense, again. Adding additional requirements that use or may minimize targeting emphasis as more Facebook users are discussed, with less precision potentially. In the UI, there is no way to select the or the operator. Facebook makes those decisions and defines them as hard presets. See this example: there are 449,740 men living in the U.S. who are 18 years of age or older and like NASCAR.

- There are 902,040 men living in the United States, being 18 years of age or older, and like NASCAR or bowling. The estimated scope has improved since now we have targeted users who like bowling or NASCAR.

- There are 2,465,440 men living in the United States, being 18 years of age or older, and like NASCAR or cooking or bowling. Estimated coverage has improved as we have now targeted users like NASCAR or cooking or bowling.

That is a critical idea. Only note that with each new targeting attribute separated by the or operator, the approximate scope is increased. Later in this chapter, as we review each targeting attribute, we will again point out which values are affected by preset or operators.

And Or Together

The whole stew becomes even more pungent when one realizes that the or-separated interests in the bucket of Interests and some other attributes work in a relationship with the other major targeted areas.

There are 112,520 women living in the U.S. and like opera. There are 7,040 women living in the USA who are interested in women and like opera. The estimated reach has been drastically reduced due to the presetting between the Demographics (where gender is chosen) and Advanced Demographics (where sexual preference is chosen) sections and operator. Note, the filters refine, and allows user-wide combinations of targeting attributes and thus reduce scope.

There are 37,640 women living in the U.S. who are interested in women and like opera or classical music. The approximate scope has been expanded by presetting the server or user in the Interests bucket (where interests are chosen). Note, the scope or operator can, and slightly decreases emphasis in this situation. That is important. We didn't find gay women who like both opera and classical music. We like both opera and classical music. If the additional section had either been Opera's Phantom or Pavarotti, emphasis may not have been reduced, as both are highly related to "Opera." Start with the basic premise. The main sections have the and operator between them: Location Demographics Interests Connections on Facebook Advanced Demographics Education & Work Specifying values in any of these main sections decreases reach because targeted users must meet all the criteria in each section in combination. Think of each segment as having performance targeting determined by selections made to the attributes within.

Several targeting criteria are strung together by the main sections, and others by or. Hang inside. You will get it as we discuss every attribute within each main section. It might be time you started listening to music while you were reading.

Typing Patterns Reveal Related Segments

All through the UI, all qualities for each attribute box are preset. Typing a word in any UI box that isn't a piccc of Facebook's preset social diagram essentially won't bring about a worth that Facebook Ads will acknowledge for targeting.

Luckily for advertisers, FB goes to excellent lengths to reveal social fragments that are thoughtfully identified with distinct words composed into the UI. This usefulness is a supernatural occurrence of current contextual targeting. For example, typing the Boston Bruins into the Precise Interests attributes box presents choices that I never would have thought of.

A touch of facilitated alphanumeric example testing encompassing key ideas yields entrancing UI typing hacks. These typing patterns help reveal a cornucopia of preset Facebook targeting attributes accessible to browse. Consider it a similar path as an inquiry and-salvage crucial by the coast monitor, scouring the ocean in a network to find a missing boat. You actually type patterns to the point that a beat is set up. To the favored barely any offered access to the Facebook Ads application programming interface (API), these testing lattices can be computerized. For all of you advertisers out there, become acclimated to the possibility of those typing patterns.

This is effectively outlined in its most fundamental structure by typing the letter an in the Precise Interests pail. The accompanying preset social-portions stock is offered: A Prayer For Owen Meany, A Clockwork Orange, A Walk to Remember, Aaron, etc. They appear to be generally offered by portion size, yet this is a long way from reliable. To investigate b, backspace and type the letter.

It works for words, as well, not simply singular letters. Start with the word boat in the Interests container. Boats, Boating, Boat book, Boat That Rocked, and Boat Trip are the main choices.

That is extraordinary, some acceptable choices without a doubt, yet apparently arbitrary. Facebook doesn't reveal its calculation for how it selects. One can just envision.

From the nuts and bolts, things can just get increasingly confounded as the inquiry patterns develop. Summon a little cunning. Take a stab at typing in a boat, the a being the main letter of an in sequential order search design intended to find progressively social fragments not indicated beforehand.

Presently we're getting someplace. Pieces of intrigue—gold like Antique Boat Center, Andros Boatworks, and Aberdeen Boat Club Hong Kong are rendered. Attempt boat c, boat d, or boat 1 to tissue out considerably progressively preset targeting thoughts. To travel through the various tests quicker, duplicate boat to your PC's Clipboard.

- Paste boat/type a space and an after boat/select any presets.

- Paste boat/type a space and b after boat/select any presets.

- Paste boat/type a space and c after boat/select any presets.

When preset choices have been found, selected, and depleted, embrace a similar testing design utilizing firmly related words, which can incorporate plurals, condensing, and equivalent words:

- Paste boats/select any presets.

- Paste boats/type a space and a/select any presets.

- Paste boats/type a space and b/select any presets.

- Paste boats/type a space and c/select any presets, and so forth.

- Paste yacht/select any presets.

- Paste yacht/type a space and a/select any presets.

- Paste yacht/type a space and b/select any presets, and so forth.

- Paste yachts/select any presets.

- Paste yachts/type a space and a/select any presets.

- Paste yachts/type a space and b/select any presets, and so forth.

Each targeting attribute has its own particular alpha patterns, which can be utilized to hack out up to this time unrevealed preset choices. Some typing patterns are progressively Byzantine and others require some inventiveness. We'll investigate great patterns as we spread each attribute.

Note: Facebook Ads targeting just perceives alphanumeric characters for targeting. "Amazon.com" becomes "amazoncom" and "I <3" (text saying for "heart" or "love") becomes "I 3".

Location

The principal main section of the targeting module is Location. The act of geotargeting ads is respected and demonstrated. When you've selected the country or countries you'd prefer to target, it's easy to additionally refine the crowd by selecting specific states, provinces, or cities users self-identify as their location. Just locations that are inside your selected countries will bc shown.

Facebook Ads' geotargeting is a more profound creature than the great IP-driven geotargeting search pay-per-click advertisers have come to know throughout the years. Web indexes regularly mine a user's Internet Protocol (IP) address to accommodate location against a database of IP addresses and physical locations, including countries and cities. Facebook bases its geotargeting, generally, on the location users guarantee when rounding out their Facebook profiles.

As indicated by Facebook, "If a user has listed a present location on their profile, they may see ads targeted to that location, paying little heed to where they are as of now found. Ads are not targeted to a user's geographic networks or some other information." Marketers are not given controls to pick between targeting users by either IP location or addresses in their profiles. Facebook decides off camera.

It's stunning how precise this truly is: It can tell when you're away and places ads from that area on your page. Facebook decides and appears to make an average showing understanding the distinction between an excursion and a changeless move.

Facebook Mobile has been widely adopted. The 200 million dynamic users getting to FB by means of their cell phones are two times more dynamic than non-versatile users. This forecasts a mind-boggling future for advertisers, who could profit by adding extra geographic context to targeting.

Facebook Places, a profoundly announced versatile application much like Foursquare, encourages users to "check-in" at an Event Page or organizations' Places pages. Clearly, users give away profoundly specific geolocation information, developed by their cell phones' GPS signals. If widely adopted by users, this could be a fortune trove of hot-live information that is sufficiently transient to give information important to advertisers.

For example, if a promoter could target users checked in at a specific Laundromat, conceivably with time to kill while garments dry, the users could be targeted by a coffeehouse nearby contribution free espresso for Laundromat benefactors. It's not right now conceivable to target Facebook Ads by this strategy. Notwithstanding, it is now conceivable to "target individuals who 'Like' your Place page if you have played out a Page to Place converge," as per Facebook. This appears to convey similar impediments of Facebook Page promoting, where advertisers are permitted to target just their own fans, companions of their own fans, or everybody except their own fans.

Later on, we might have the option to target by blends of user profile and IP address concoction, and simply think about the potential outcomes! It would be super-cool to target people who live in Montreal, as showed by their Places exercises while visiting Nantucket. These users may be targeted by ads that tout uncommon Canadian money trade rates at an establishment in Nantucket.

Country

The principal attribute in the Location section is Country, which defaults to the country you register as home. This attribute is obligatory so as to push ahead—if you deselect all passages in the Country section, the estimated reach isn't zero be that as it may, technically, invalid. Picking a country is extremely direct. Like all Facebook Ads parameters, countries are preset values that populate as you type. You can't simply type in the letters for some country that Facebook doesn't offer as a preset. Facebook doesn't have an All Countries setting, and you're constrained to targeting 25 countries one after another. Not to worry; for the following reasons for existing, it's about constantly a superior plan to target littler gatherings or single countries in a single advertisement.

Research-Typing Pattern One

Type an in the Country parameter box to see 26 countries starting with a. Facebook lets us target from Afghanistan to the United Arab Emirates. Type in al to see the countries starting with these two letters: Aland Islands, Albania, and Algeria. This research-typing design works in various other Facebook Ads parameters boxes.

Picking multiple countries takes out the choice to target specific states and provinces inside those countries. To target specific states and provinces inside multiple countries, make multiple ads targeted to every one of the countries, each in turn.

Off-camera, Facebook Ads embeds the or administrator between multiple countries, which means targeted users live in any of the countries listed. While a few users may have double citizenship or guarantee multiple homes (think college understudies concentrating abroad), you can't target such duplicity in the Country attribute box. For useful applications, each extra country adds more users to the countries container.

State and Province

If accessible, based on selecting a country, the following attribute in the Location section in State and Province. If a solitary country is sufficiently large as well as it really has states, provinces, or comparable to subdivided regions, ticking the states and province's radio catch reveals granular states and province's choices.

In reality, not all countries allude to their regions like states or provinces. The way to making sense of how every country works on Facebook is to perceive what attribute boxes appear after country selection and what preset values are returned. Generally, the UI is naturally powerful and verges on dealing with various country arrangements. Some stuff doesn't bode well, so make certain to focus. The United Kingdom is really a protected government and unitary state, not a country. Wales is technically a country inside the UK. However in Facebook Ads, UK is a country and Wales appears as a state, however, Wales isn't technically a state.

Pick the Northern Mariana Islands and watch the State and Province choices vanish. Simply remember that in Facebook Ads, states and provinces have different setups, dealt with in grouped ways, including concealing city as well as state parameters and different workarounds for less basic governmental assignments.

City

Another location-based choice to refine your targeting is to select specific cities. Just cities inside the selected countries will be shown. The Cities parameter box is super-cool. It's shrewd as well. Picking multiple countries takes out the Cities choice, which means advertisers can't target the United States/New York and London/United Kingdom in the equivalent targeting situation. To achieve this, copy the promotion, targeting each clone to an alternate country/city blend.

Picking cities is easy. Simply begin typing the name and the rest will deal with itself Don't be astonished if a specific city someplace isn't listed. Facebook isn't all over, however it sometimes appears that way. Another intriguing element is the capacity to target users inside 10-, 25-, or 50-mile ranges of selected cities. Since it works for more than one city, this capacity makes drawing hovers around an assortment or populace focus an extremely helpful strategy.

Socioeconomics: Age and Sex

Next up is to determine the age scope of users you'd prefer to target. Facebook proposes beginning wide and narrowing down based on the age consequences of starting impressions and clicks.

For sex, indicate whether your advertisement should target the two sexual orientations, just men, or just women. Remember that a few users don't identify their sex and can be reached just if you select All. This clarifies an undeniable error. Men in addition to women don't indicate All. This is an issue overall targeting criteria with the exception of the country since users aren't at present required to enter all targeting criteria. This is one of only a handful of hardly any shortcomings of Facebook targeting. Not to worry. Most users give the information up.

With regards to some advertisement content encompassing contraception, sex training, wellbeing conditions, dating destinations, and related substance or administrations, ads must be targeted distinctly to users 18 years old or more established. Likewise, the Interested In targeting parameter must be applied, and a solitary estimation of either Men or Women selected.

Broad and Exact Age Match

The age parameter defaults to Broad Match in the Demographics main section, meaning users are also targeted just outside the defined age range. The ads may be viewed by users who are 18 and 25 in the scenario where the ages of 19 to 24 are selected. It's cheaper for a big match. Facebook provides an undisclosed reduction in cost per press, in return for allowing reduced emphasis in choosing targeted ages. A wide age match is chosen by unchecking the Require Exact Age Match button. By doing so, you grant Facebook permission to offer your advertisements to those within the age range defined, as well as to those who fall slightly outside the range but at a discounted price.

If you check the Require Exact Age Matchbox, basically you pay more for Facebook to target only users within the age range you specify. Anyone outside the age range will never receive the ads, no matter how well all the other targeting lines up. Facebook explains: "By allowing the system to increase the delivery of your ads slightly outside your target age range, you can get additional discounted impressions and clicks that are generally just as valuable as the impressions and clicks within your target age." In some geographic locations, although age selection may still be possible in the UI, age targeting may actually be neutralized. Facebook maintains that, at certain locations, it does not "serve ads to any Facebook user within certain age groups. The user interface of Facebook Ads may allow you to set up advertisements targeting that age group, but Facebook won't deliver those advertising. "According to Facebook TOS, other forms of advertisement may not be offered to children under the age of 18, including advertising for dating sites and alcoholic beverages. In the United States, the Childhood Online Protection Act (COPA) restricts the dissemination of "harmful content to children," described as material that is considered to pique "prurient interest" by "contemporary community standards," including displaying sexual acts or nudity. This is a quality far broader than the obscenity. One believes that FB is receptive to COPA requirements, and complies with them.

World-Famous Interests Bucket

The official name of this targeting attribute has changed over the past three years from "Keyword" to "Likes and Interests" this year to "Precise Interests." We lovingly refer to the next major section of the targeting UI as the Interests bucket or Interests bucket. If one parameter box exemplifies the targeting cornucopia of Facebook in abundance, it is the bucket of Interests. The internal algorithm parsing the social graph of Facebook for presets in this box is so incredibly powerful that we sometimes refer to each interest as a "social segment." From foot fetishes to cupcake baking, this section is where the targeting rubber meets the social graphic road. As we move forward, we're going to refer to Precise Interests targeting attribute as the Interest Bucket, because that's what it is. Adding additional likes and interests to this bucket doesn't mean that users are filtered down to those interested in Interest #1 and Interest #2 in combination. Alternatively, the or operator is placed in the bucket of Interests between parameters.

Here's an example: If values are Basket Weaving and Botany in the Interests bucket, we are targeting users interested in either basket weaving or botany. In your own view, insert the or operator in between interests while adding more likes and interests to the bucket of Interests.

New advertisers to Facebook Ads also wonder why Facebook only provides the or operator within the bucket of Interests. Wouldn't Facebook's adding a and option in the Interests bucket be an easy math feature? Many believe the answer to that question is twofold. Firstly, the sampling of users was much smaller when the UI was developed. Allowing marketers to weave and target intricate people revealing users who like this and that and those could quickly reduce to barely any of the available users. Even when there were 50 million users in the Facebook population, the sampling was not broad enough to support such a micro-targeting idea.

More likely now that Facebook has about 700 million users, it could be a privacy nightmare to offer the and operator as an option between interests in the bucket of Interests. Imagine if we could target users who work at Best Buy, who lives in Minnesota, who are 19 to 21 years old, go to Minnesota University, such as teachers and educators, and pot or marijuana, or foot fetish. The FCC would crawl up Facebook's snoot with a microscope and the current dialogue on privacy would rage out of control even further. Still, it is a titillating prospect. It's a moot point because within the Like bucket we don't get the and the operator. It is safe to say that one of the most important political decisions in marketing history is defined by a tiny word: or not and in the bucket of Interest.

Note: "Likes," "Interests," and "Likes & Interests" nomenclature opens a can of worms and inconsistent language throughout FB ads. This attribute is called "Interests" in the Web UI, and is subdivided into either "Precise Interests" or "Specific Category Targeting." Power Editor refers to this attribute as "Likes & Interests." The Web UI's "Estimated Reach" target description box uses the word "Like," while Power Editor has no summary.

Interests, Bucketed Intent

In search marketing, we invest a lot of energy putting forth a valiant effort to connect keywords with intent, or what the user truly needs to achieve. Without a doubt, the catchphrase food provider is handily extrapolated to cooking. Get a thesaurus and it won't take long to stem outward to find food support or even party-arranging. Be that as it may, the watchword gourmet food delivery Manhattan is entirely attractive on the grounds that the words the user-selected obviously uncover intent. Delivery most likely methods the user needs to purchase now. Gourmet means a client with better tastes, may be amenable to buying an increasingly costly item. Manhattan reveals the location, yet additionally aggravates the sense of availability to purchase.

In social segments, as in search keywords, users' intent is regularly revealed, that is, the thing that sorts of items would at any rate register or, best case scenario, truly get their eyes and provoke feelings. Continuously ask, "What might we be able to offer to users interested in X, Y, or Z?"

If at any time there was a spot to communicate inventiveness, intuition, and cunning, the Interests bucket is it. Marketing on

Facebook requires an entirely different sense of amusingness than some other channel requires. All things considered, we're not targeting keywords that users search. Or maybe, we're knee-somewhere down in contextual or stroll by space. Consider picking social segments that characterize clients' attributes, how they live life, communicate, tithe, what they read, brands expended, political tendencies, pioneers followed, corruptions, sufferings, callings, pastimes, and numerous different inclinations, tastes, and affinities.

Social marketing requires magnificently sideways reasoning. For example sweatbands and water jugs to the 1,218,560 people who live in the United States; are age 18 or more established; and like tennis educator, tennis, playing tennis, I appreciate playing tennis, Sanwa tennis foundation, tennis club, tennis trainer, I love tennis, tennis life camps, we love tennis, tennis expert, tennis player, or tennis runs in our blood.

Sometimes, targeting can be somewhat not so much obscure but rather more exacting, despite the fact that we're working in contextual space. Might you be able to sell Rosetta Stone language learning programming to an estimated reach of 15,980 people who live in the United States, are age 30 or more established, and like learning Arabic, learning Italian, learning Spanish, communicating in Spanish, learning french, learning to communicate in French, learning Hebrew, learning Portuguese, or learning Russian?

Interests starting from the drop box that shows up as you type will target your ads to users that list at least one of those things on their profiles. Facebook reminds advertisers: "Not all users complete these fields, so picking fields here will constrain the targeting of your ads to just those users with at least one of these Interests."

Social Synonyms: Getting from Here to There

It's fascinating that the most ideal approach to convey social segments is as yet communicated by keywords, despite the fact that it's not questions that trigger Facebook ads. In this manner, when managing the Interests bucket, keep the inborn connection among keywords and social segments in mind. Synonyms are absolutely your companion. Microsoft Word's inline thesaurus is a magnificent starter apparatus to help uncover "social synonyms." We likewise use UrbanDictionary.com a lot to discover slang that is frequently pervasive on Facebook.

Take the case of marketing an überhealthy granola bar with reused bundling to a target crowd containing Facebook users who care about sustainable living. It's easy to comprehend targeting 29,900 people who live in Australia, New Zealand, Canada, United States, United Kingdom, or Ireland; they are age 24 and more established; and like sustainable earth, sustainable living, sustainable food Denver, or sustainable food.

Presently put on your semantic cap, snatch the thesaurus in some structure, and giddyup with equivalent word disclosure. It won't take long to discover natural and organic. We're going to run a typing pattern in the Interests bucket. Start the process by making a list of every conceivable mix of our root social equivalent word affiliations. The reason here is to debilitate each conceivable social segment:

organic food

natural food

- Put on your typing fingers and execute the accompanying pattern:

- Type organic food/duplicate organic food/select any presets that apply.

- Paste organic food/select any presets that apply.

- Paste organic food select any presets continue until there are not anymore applicable segments to choose.

- Type natural food/duplicate natural food/select any presets that apply.

- Paste natural food/select any presets that apply.

- Paste natural food select any presets continue until there are not any more applicable segments to choose from.

The estimated reach for this segment is 156,900 people who live in the United States, are age 19 and more seasoned, and like organic food, organic foods, natures way organic foods, homegrown organic neighbourhood food coop, natural foods, natural food association, sways red factory natural foods, brazos natural foods, crude food naturals, oryana natural foods showcase, grows natural foods bistro, natural foods, or rock gorge natural foods.

It's cool to take note of that we've found Facebook users who like organic and natural food, yet in addition are likewise interested in specific bistros, other food brands, and Whole Foods–sorts of general stores. It's easy to perceive how regarding social segments as keywords, making sense of synonyms in the semantic world, and circling the synonyms through the Facebook intrigue bucket can yield fantastic outcomes. We advise our group to "consistently reclassify the box that is no joke."

This technique is extraordinary, however organic food is a moderately long tail space in Facebook, in that there are not tremendous pockets of intrigue. That is the reason all we needed to do was paste the major two-word mixes to locate the cool stuff that applied. Shorter tail space, where there are, indeed, enormous measures of users interested in things, require more discretion in figuring out what is relevant and increasingly serious finger technique to run the hunt matrix.

State the assignment is to advertise College GameDay Fan Gear to football lovers all things considered. To start with, typing the word football in the Interests bucket results in recommended interests. We should step back for a moment. Football really implies soccer in many spots, however for the most part not in the U.S. We as it cared about clear American turf football interests. Since we're in the U.S., we'll go with the greater part of the suggestions, except for England Football. Check the suggestions you acknowledge and hit invigorates suggestions to check whether there are any progressively clear ones.

The following suggestions are about England—Pro Evo, England Football, Match Of The Day, Liverpool Football Club, Soccer Am, and England Football Team, so we'll pass and move along.

Duplicate football onto your PC Clipboard.

Paste football/select any segments relevant to your marketing. Presently we've included football industrial facility, football match-ups, football time Tennessee, football manager 2009, football recordings, or football season.

- Paste football/type a space and a/select any segments relevant to your marketing. Rehash this process until applicable segments are depleted.

- Paste football/type a space and stomach muscle/select any segments relevant to your marketing.

- Paste football/type a space and air conditioning/select any segments relevant to your marketing.

- Paste football/type a space and advertisement/select any segments relevant to your marketing.

- Paste football/type a space and ae/select any segments relevant to your marketing.

- Paste football/type a space and af/select any segments relevant to your marketing.

Continue the pattern until each of the two-letter blends for the letter a have been tested. If you would prefer not to test each and every letter, the undeniable second letters to test with an eventual consonant. Simply think carefully. If the primary letter is a consonant, the undeniable second letters to test would be vowels.

This technique works admirably of testing all words related to your main catchphrase. It takes an advertiser's discretion to select just segments and recommended segments that apply to the marketing jobs needing to be done.

Going above and beyond, typing the initial three letters of the subsequent word is once in a while justified however sometimes worth the jag. In the football contextual investigation, typing football shows Football Sunday and Football Sundays. Well. I wonder if there's a whole other world to that. Obviously, there is. In the realm of American games, Sundays are for all intents and purposes gospel, holy, the Sabbath.

Type football sun. Lo and view, presently we've included Sunday Funday Football Fans, Sunday football, Sun football, Sunday Night Football on NBC, Watching football on Sunday, and Joey Doyles football Sunday. Had we not followed our intuition and worked with the third letter, a fortune trove of football targets would have been missed.

General classification targeting permits you to reach

gatherings of people who share comparable interests and attributes. These classes draw from the real information people have remembered for their profiles, permitting you to effortlessly reach your optimal crowd. Peruse and select from our list of classes to begin.

Broad Categories Targeting

As recently mentioned, Facebook is well known for tossing spaghetti at the divider (no play on words expected) in that they test, refine, or even expel critical devices with little pomp. As of this composition, FB has been testing a Broad Category highlight to target preset user bunches sharing normal segment attributes. Your Facebook Ads record might possibly approach this targeting device. If it does, you'll see a Switch to Broad Category Targeting join simply under the Interests attribute, as shown in. To switch out of Broad Category mode, click Switch to Precise Interest Targeting.

General classification targeting lets promotes train in on users who, as FB would like to think, share related interests and attributes. The Facebook Ads help section states that "these categories draw from the genuine information people have remembered for their profiles, permitting you to effortlessly reach your optimal crowd."

Our tests show that these presets are powerful and, sometimes, offer access to specific socioeconomics that are in any case hard to target with a high level of specificity, utilizing the exemplary Interests bucket each segment in turn. Simply look that it is so easy to target guardians who are bringing up kids among birth and three years of age, Cool! That particular targeting assignment would be about incomprehensible utilizing the Precise

Interest Targeting alternative.

Different categories appear to be progressively emotional. For example, in the United States, comprehensively targeting Retail/Luxury Goods brings about fingering around 5 million users. What precisely does that mean? FB doesn't let us know without a doubt. It is safe to say that they are targeting people who perused Condé Nast magazines or are interested in Rolex watches? Obscure. My point is that, for a portion of these categories, I'd preferably make sense of the segments myself, utilizing Precise Interests Targeting instead of utilizing FB's presets.

In any case, the Broad Category instrument shows a guarantee if FB keeps it around. If it's not too much trouble note that this element isn't steady yet and we've seen it added to accounts just to see it expelled from a few and not others. All things considered, the abilities are noteworthy enough that they bear mention.

Outer Semantic Stemming Tools

In the watchword research universe, we call the thesaurus work stemming. Microsoft Word's thesaurus is just one of the numerous devices we use to stem keywords. Here's a look at aimClear's preferred apparatuses:

WordTracker, Lateral Stemming Thesaurus: www.wordtracker.com.

Google AdWords Keyword Tool: https://adwords.google.com/select/KeywordToolExternal. Attempt expression and wide match.

Trellian Keyword Discovery: www.keyworddiscovery.com.

Wikipedia can be a magnificent spot to stem keywords for synonyms—have a go at following the path from the interlinking in articles.

YouTube, Google, and Bing search recommendation boxes. Utilize the ScrapeBox application (for Windows just) to effectively explore them in one UI: www.scrapebox.com.

Propelled Demographics

The Advanced Demographics section is entirely sexy. There are no ifs and or buts. Channel by sexuality, workplace, relationship status, and languages spoken, and even point ads at people on their birthday.

Birthday

Birthday targeting permits ads to be targeted to users on their birthdays. With this alternative, advertisers can make exceptionally relevant ads or highlight special offers accessible to users on their birthdays.

This current one's easy. Checking Target People On Their Birthdays does only that, inside the limits of the general targeting picture. Facebook proposes that "advertisers can make exceptionally relevant ads or highlight special offers accessible to users on their birthdays." Right on, at that point!

Showing ads to this targeting technique for a course of days results in serving ads to users whose birthdays happen on the specific day the ads run. Facebook users with April 14 birthdays will see birthday-targeted ads just on April 14. Running the battle over the 15th and sixteenth outcomes in users praising their special days on the 15th and sixteenth seeing the promotion.

Tip: Facebook doesn't give understanding with respect to what different ads exist for any social segment. Wondering what different advertisers are likewise targeting certain interests or different attributes? View your own live ads or contenders' ads basically by briefly changing your own Facebook profile. For knowledge concerning what advertisers are targeting, incidentally, change your own Facebook profile's interests. Despite the fact that it disregards Facebook terms of administrations, a few advertisers make a shadow profile only for this reason. Take a stab at changing your birthday to the present schedule day or adjusting different parts of your profile. Remember to test for geo-targeted ads by changing your old neighborhood.

Relationship Status and Sexuality

Through their profile, people show their sexual interests. Although it's not needed, during account setup and profile maintenance several people happily put out for Facebook's queries. If the privacy settings publicly display it is easy to see if users are interested in men, women or both. When confidentiality settings are locked, all that does is hide information from other users. It does not exclude advertisers from marketing to those preferences on Facebook ads. Such knowledge will telegraph lucrative marketplaces, or users with internal contradictions, in combination with other elements.

Under Relationship, you can address any or all of those

identifying as Single, In A Relationship, Engaged, or Married. Some users don't specify their relationship status and can be reached only if you choose All.

Under the Interested In Demographic, you can segment by sexual preference. Choose whether your advertising will reach all users or only users who are interested in men or women. Some users do not specify this information, like the relationship status, and can therefore only be reached if you select All.

Straight up, here are American out - of-the-closet Facebook gay men, some of whom may or may not have an accent: there are 122,940 people living in the United States who are 18 years of age or older; they are in a relationship; they speak English (US), English (UK), English (Pirate), French (France), French (Canada), Spanish (Spain), or Hungarian; and they are interested in men.

What does a person say about sexual interest? There are many different opinions. Classic marketing claims gay people have more disposable cash because, on average, there are fewer kids in the family. Marketing to engaged women obviously has certain markets. Here are some other noteworthy groups with distinct interests: there are 7,900 women living in the United States; they are 18 years of age or older; such as vegetarianism, vegetarian, vegetarian cooking, vegetarian vitamins, vegetarian food, vegetarian nutrition, or rock vegetarians; and women: gay female vegetarians.

There are 3,166,760 men (girls) living either in the United States or in Canada; they are 13 years old; they are single; and they are interested in women: the love of teen boys.

There are 10,480 people living in the United States; 18 years of age or older; like a republican party, a democrat, a republican conservative, a Republican conservative, a republican GOP, a conservative Republican, a conservative republican, a very conservative republican or a republican conservative party; and men: gay male republicans.

There are 21,640 men living in the United States; they are 18 years of age or older; such as equal rights change, equal rights, equal marriage rights for all, gay rights media, gay rights support, gay rights support, NSW gay lesbian rights lobby, gay civil rights movement, international gay lesbian human rights commission, defeat proposal 8, repeal prop8, prop 8 being overturned, stop prop 8 or inspired.

There are 2,540 women living in the United States; they are 18 years of age or older; such as construction, construction manager, construction worker, construction worker, or highway construction worker; and are interested in women: gay construction workers.

Remember to check Facebook Ads Guidelines because some products have certain targeting requirements that we have previously described. Simply put, advertisers should target only users over the age of 18 who have indicated that they are single for dating services while selling most of the adult-themed products and services.

Languages

Enter that language in the Languages box if you wish to target individuals using Facebook in a language other than the common language for the selected location. When you leave this field blank, your ads will target all users, regardless of the language they use on Facebook, at the specified location.

Languages transcend geographical boundaries, remember. There are more than 30 million people who speak English not living in the United States, the United Kingdom or Canada. Check the different languages to significantly broaden marketplaces in different countries.

Education and Work

The Education and Work section gives a brilliant layer of

trendy core interest. We have a few customers who have attempted a years-long technique of delicately marketing to tomorrow's idea heads. Target users by colleges joined in, territories of projects and courses, and graduation year, including graduated class. Since Facebook began at Harvard and afterward spread, from the start, among Ivy League schools, at that point all colleges, and afterward secondary schools, there are a lot of cool treats here. Consolidate instruction attributes with self-detailed occupations in the Interests bucket to come up with an intense shaker of uptown targeting.

To target users who are at a specific instructive level—college graduate, in college, or in secondary school—select the proper attribute. Something else, select All to target all users paying little heed to instruction.

To target users at a specific organization or association, enter the name of the workplace in the Workplaces field. Something else, leave this clear.

Element boxes open automatically when a few options are selected. Selecting College Grad or In College opens the College and Majors boxes, as recently portrayed.

It's really clear that FB doesn't offer us the capacity to select specific secondary schools as a result of the drag factor. That is most likely a smart thought.

Here are some targeting situations for your feasting and moving delight. We'll start with Boston-region college understudies who don't list the United States as their home, at any rate in their Facebook profiles. You get the image.

This first segment, delineates the volume of Facebook users who list a country other than the U.S. as their present country of living arrangement yet learn at a college in Boston, Massachusetts, and list English as a language they talk:

- There are 3,700 people who live in either Canada, United Kingdom, Australia, Japan, China, France, Mexico, or Ireland; are age 18 or older; are at BU, Boston Conservatory, BC, Boston Baptist College, Boston College for Professional Studies, Boston Institute, Boston Computer Institute, Harvard, MIT, MCPHS, Mass. Art, or Mass Maritime; and communicate in English (US), English (UK), English (Pirate), or English (Upside Down).

- There are 4,940 people who live in the United States; are at Illinois, Indiana, University of Iowa, Michigan, Michigan, State University, University of Minnesota, UNL, Northwestern, Ohio State, Purdue, Wisconsin, or

Penn State; and are majoring in mechanical designing.

- There are 680 people who live in the United States; are age 18 or older; are at BYU, Notre Dame, Wheaton IL, Grove City, Hillsdale, Bethel IN, Azusa, Pacific, Evangel, Biola, Palm Beach Atlantic University, Judson University, Bethel MN, or Judson AL; and are majoring in vocal execution, music organization, music execution, theatre arts, theatre move, theatre arts, performing arts, compelling artwork, studio art, media arts, expressive arts, or art studio.

- There are 200 people who live in the United States; they are age 18 and older; they are at Brown, Columbia, Cornell, Dartmouth, Harvard, Princeton, UPenn, or Yale; and are majoring in uncertain.

- There are 520 people who live in the United States; are age 18 or older; are at Cal Poly, CSU Northridge, CSU Fullerton, CSU Long Beach, Cal Poly, Pomona, CSU Chico, CSU Sacramento, CSU Fresno, California PA, CSU San Marcos, Humboldt State, S.F. State, San Diego State, San Diego, San Diego Christian, UCSD, Point Loma, Alliant, CA Western, Art Institute of California - San Diego, Thomas Jefferson School of Law, SF

Conservatory, San Francisco Art Inst., San Francisco School of Digital Filmmaking, University of San Francisco, Academy of Art, Universidad Francisco de Paula Santander, CA College of the Arts, Uni San Francisco de Quito, UC Hastings, San Jose State, or San Jose City College; and are majoring in communicate news coverage, correspondence news coverage, correspondence media, broad communications, or media contemplates.

The Workplaces element absolutely doesn't record each organization. Truth be told, it's a quite short tail. All things considered, it has been developing for quite a long time, directly along with Facebook itself. Utilize your great alpha pattern practice, sometimes up to four letters. You know the drill:

For a preview of the element's profundity:

Type an and see.

Type al and see.

Type all and see.

Type all and see.

Type all and see. Allan Industries is currently obvious, however, was not until the initial four letters were typed.

There are 11,500 people who live in the United States in Minnesota, California or Texas; are age 18 or older; and work, best case scenario Buy.

There are 2,600 people who live in the United Kingdom, are age 18 or older, and work at UK Parliament.

There are 17,760 people who live in the United States and work at Delta Air Lines.

The force and complexities of the Education and Work device add a wonderful dimension to Facebook Ads. Utilized in shrewd pair with the other main sections, each present and administrator in the middle of, it's easy to characterize personas for advertisers.

Associations on Facebook

Facebook permits you to target users who have just communicated enthusiasm for your Facebook content... or not. The options are straightforward and ground-breaking.

Target Users Who Are Connected

The primary target-by-connections option is to target users who are as of now "connected" to your Facebook assets. This means they've engaged your content, for instance by "loving" your page, RSVPing to your event, joining your group, or cooperating with your app. Start typing in the target field and watch as it populates with these Facebook assets you've recently made.

Targeting users who are mindful of your brand as well as burrow it and engage with it loans certain chances. Consider fitting promotion duplicate that addresses them as VIP members or esteemed clients, and offer special coupons or different motivating forces selective to your current audience. Facebook recommends leaving this field blank except if you will likely specifically target, or narrow, an audience comprising just of people previously connected to your page, group, event, or app.

All things considered, these capacities are accessible just to owners and directors of FB pages, groups, and apps. At the end of the day, I can't choose to target the entirety of Starbucks' fans by this attribute. I can likely find a workable pace different means, in any case—for instance, by means of the Interests bucket.

Target Users Who Are Not Connected

Alternately, the second targeting option for connections narrows your audience to incorporate just users who are not effectively connected to your Facebook properties—at the end of the day, users who have not yet engaged with your content (they don't "prefer" your page, have never been welcome to an event, haven't joined your group, or haven't associated with your app). To target these users, follow a similar technique as in the past— start typing in the target field and select the Facebook properties you need to indicate.

Targeting users who are not effectively connected to your brand's quality on Facebook additionally gives one of a kind chances, for example, publicizing with the intent of selecting new members, fans, or clients or offering limited time limits for first-time customers. Facebook recommends leaving this field blank except if your intent is to narrow your target audience to people not effectively connected to your brand. Once more, these targeting rights are accessible just to owners and administrators.

Target Users Whose Friends Are Connected

The third and last approach to target by connections is to channel your audience for users whose friends are connected to your page, event, group, or application. Same as in the past, simply enter the name of your Facebook element in the field and select the properties whereupon you need to centre.

Concocting ads that address this second-degree targeted audience can ostensibly require more sideways intuition than the initial two target-by-connections options. Think about pulling that first-level of partition—the user's friend who as of now enjoys your page, group, etc—into the promotion. Something like, "Hello—your friend likes [product]! Perhaps you will, as well!" or "Do your friends love [product]? Get them the latest version for these special seasons!" may grab their attention and plant a thought in their mind.

Promotion Targeting Options Help Center

If all else fails, Facebook's Help Center is great. The Ads: Targeting Options section, which can be found at www.facebook.com/help/?page=863, is a particularly valuable asset for a wide exhibit of questions running from the fundamental (what is birthday targeting?) to the marginally further developed (what are the advantages of refining my targeting as opposed to attempting to reach a more extensive audience?).

The contents right now offered in over a dozen languages, including English, Italian, Turkish, Spanish, German, French, and Portuguese. There are additionally in-line help things inside Facebook assigned by little dim question marks alongside specific elements in the UI. Between this book, the assistance section, and that in-line understanding, you ought to be genuinely repaired.

CHAPTER SEVEN

Campaigns, Pricing, and Scheduling

The third step, in the wake of planning the ads and targeting users, is about coordinations to bid, timetable, and document the ad inside campaigns. Facebook Ads offers to estimate and planning options normal to current online ad stages. There are a couple of intriguing peculiarities, however it is in any case clear.

To begin with, make another campaign or choose a current one. Beside association, having separate campaigns is significant in light of the fact that you can assign a budget for each. Choose either an every day or lifetime campaign budget. Choosing an everyday budget disperses that campaign's ad spend consistently. Choosing a lifetime budget conveys the ad spend all through the length of the campaign. Check the "Run my campaign ceaselessly starting today" box and ads will run at max speed until the budget is exhausted, instead of the budget being metered out over the campaign time frame.

Next, select the calendar by choosing starting and consummation dates. If you checked the "Run my campaign ceaselessly starting today" box, the completion date will be turned grey out on the grounds that the campaign closes when you come up short on cash. It's intriguing to take note of that choosing an everyday budget with persistent running does at present dark out the end date, so you need to make sure to kill the campaign when you need it to stop.

CPC versus CPM

Facebook Ads offer two payment model decisions, cost per click (CPC) and cost per thousand impressions (CPM). Impressions mean times the ad is shown. Choosing CPC means that each click, up to the amount you've bid, will be charged against your budget. To my mind, this is quite often the right decision. Choosing CPM means that a portion of your budget will be charged each time your ad is shown. Faccbook proposes, "This is the best decision if you'd prefer to expand brand mindfulness by users essentially observing your ad." Frankly, I don't concur. At the point when we brand, we typically still choose CPC and meter clicks by not having a call to activity in the ad, bid level, and different strategies.

Despite the charging strategy, Facebook chooses the "best ad to run based on ad execution." In my experience, FB doesn't give every ad a sufficient possibility in revolution to truly decide. In the case of utilizing CPC or CPM, the amount charged will never surpass your budget.

Evaluating

How high up on the page an ad runs, if by any means, is controlled by your bid. It's as easy as choosing the greatest amount you're willing to pay for each click or every thousand impressions. Expense is excluded from bids or budgets. Facebook proposes bids in a range, low to high . The reaches might be characteristic of the amount it will truly cost to run the ads. Without a doubt, it's a bid model, which means we're going up against others for ad situating. Notwithstanding, there are likely different variables, similar to Google AdWords quality score. Facebook doesn't reveal ad execution factors, which sway the quality score. It is most likely that bid + quality score = ad position, in rivalry with different advertisers going after position.

Use Suggested Bid (www.facebook.com/ads/make/) doesn't offer any advantage that I can decide, but to give Facebook a blank check. FB adjusts the Simple bid run upward as rivalry increments, and there is no top. Additionally, the main option is CPC, and CPM isn't accessible. The option may bode well if there were a bid-to-situate option, which may be accessible later on.

Facebook Ads' basic structure instruments, targeting lattice, and valuing options, pair with about 700 million users, amount to a mind-blowing open door for advertisers. Later in the book, we'll take a gander at advanced ad configuration, duplicate, and executioner targeting. Happy ads creation!

CHAPTER SEVEN

Facebook Ads Finances

What a Giddyup! Now that the groundwork has been laid, it is eventually time to deploy your campaign on Facebook Ads. First, though, there are a couple more factors to consider. The bids must be in a range that is sufficiently high to show the ads— the higher the ad rating (where it appears on the page), the better the click-through ratio (CTR). Facebook is a little idiosyncratic about the way advertisers are handling their budgets and are not allowed to.

Payment Options

Advertisers can pay for ads for certain currencies using Visa, MasterCard, American Express, Discover, some cobranded debit cards and JCB. Facebook offers monthly invoicing of a minimum of $10,000 a month for qualified customers. If you plan to spend $10 K or more, please contact the sales team of Facebook via the form of the Help Centre. Search Facebook Ads Help Center for more details regarding "What are my payment options?"Personally, I would like to use American Express and have my free airline tickets charged for Twitter. See, I told you that I'd make fun of that!

Facebook currently accepts the following currencies: the Australian dollar (AUD), the British pound (GBP), the Canadian dollar (CAD), the Chilean peso (CLP), the Colombian peso (COP), the euro (EUR), the Danish crown (DKK), the Hong Kong dollar (HKD), the Japanese yen (JPY), the Norwegian crown (NOK), the Swiss franc (CHF), the Turkish lira (TRY), the US dollar (USD) and the Venezuelan bolivar (VEB). Check the FB Ads support pages for "What currencies are approved for Facebook Ads, because this may change over time?"We need to create a second account to run campaigns with multiple currencies. You can keep two accounts inside your one Facebook login: one for each currency.

Budgeting and Spending Limits

For each campaign, there is a regular target that can be exceeded by two different methods The budget per day is hardwired, use-it-or-lose-it. Neither unused funds rollover.

The dynamic Lifetime Budget option. Unused funds roll forward, with Facebook setting the daily budget for each new day based on a formula that takes lifetime budget into account, how many days are on schedule, and if any unused funds are carried forward from previous days.

There are four basic financial structures to understand:

• Daily spending limit, enforced by Facebook

• Lifetime account cap, set by advertisers

• Monthly budget, set for campaigns

• Offers, set for advertisements If at first, they seem a little confusing, don't worry.
Hang in there and it is all going to make sense. I'm going to italicize a sentence at a few points. Please read that sentence again and again until you understand. I suggest you turn on Bill Evans ' "Gloria's Move (Take 2)," from the Live album at The Vanguard. Dude, music is needed in this chapter.

Daily Spend Limit and Lifetime Budget

Each account comes to set up with a general daily spend limit, which is forced by Facebook. Facebook sets the daily spend limit when you set up the account. The bad news is that new accounts default to an immaterial $50 every day, per account. "New" means the primary implementation of Facebook Ads conveyed from an account. The daily spend limit will routinely increase following a couple of days on the grounds that Facebook is fruitful at charging your Visa at each procedure level. At the point when the daily limit reaches $1,000, you'll have to contact Facebook to request further increases. All things considered, you can't raise the account-wide daily budget past what Facebook permits. You need to acquire their trust first. This can be baffling. In 2008, aimClear was running an enormous holiday campaign for Martha Stewart Omni, and for a considerable length of time, we were unable to persuade Facebook that it was cool to raise our limit over $50. Go figure.

In case you're sufficiently fortunate to have a Facebook delegate, these higher-ups can sign in to their administrative apparatuses and change the daily limit, which will produce results the following charging day. This isn't the situation for most advertisers; it isn't so easy to get a devotcd agent except if you spend oodles of cash.

You can contact Facebook's technical help by means of a web structure to request an increased limit. Try not to rely on quick reaction time, yet it will complete—eventually. Adding another cash type doesn't increase the daily limit. Or maybe, the total limit is allotted across both money accounts.

Lifetime Spend Cap

One approach to abstain from overspending in a Facebook Ads account is to set a lifetime spend cap, which assigns indisputably the absolute entirety the whole account is approved to exhaust. All ads will be stopped inside 15 minutes of when your account reaches the cap. Advertisers can reset this cap whenever, however remember that the lifetime spend limit has nothing to do with the pace of ads served. Facebook essentially delays everything when the ideal consumption limitation has been reached.

Here are the means by which you approach doing it:
1.   Head over to the Billing Manager by clicking Billing in the left-hand section.

2.   Click Edit beside your present account spend cap amount. You'll see it promptly underneath   Account Spend, which defaults to Unlimited.

3.   Enter your new account spending limit.

4.   Click Save. Alright, your lifetime budget is protected now, and you won't go over.

To start with, be cautious when setting a lifetime spend cap, and if you do, check it consistently. Here's the place things get marginally technical. Take a full breath. Each Facebook Ads account holds campaigns. Understanding the subtleties of arranging each campaign's daily budget is essential, however somewhat befuddling. Every Day, otherwise called Daily budget, and Run My Campaign Continuously Starting Today are the defaults for Facebook campaigns. Advertisers are given options to start and stop the campaign date with an everyday budget or to set a lifetime budget. Setting a lifetime budget requires a fixed time plan.

In the first place, how about we investigate Per Day, the least difficult option, in light of the fact that every day, the campaign's budget is use-it-or-lose-it. If the per-day budget is $100 and just $80 is spent on Monday, Tuesday's budget is still $100. The unused $20 doesn't turn over to increase any future day's budget. Until you're knowledgeable about Facebook Ads, Per Day is the recommended setting since it's easy to conceptualize.

Setting a campaign's lifetime budget and its related time plan approves Facebook to decide the campaign's daily budget by partitioning the lifetime budget by the quantity of days in the timetable. For experienced users, this can be a super-cool option provided that the campaign doesn't spend to its normal daily limit on Monday, Facebook will endeavor to utilize the remaining daily ad spend on Tuesday, etc. At the end of the day, unused bits of daily budgets move forward. It ought to be noted, in any case, that paying little mind to this recipe, the account's daily limit and the lifetime spending cap (that is, the limits forced by Facebook, not you) won't be surpassed in any circumstance.

Whew, that was some really dry stuff, but basic develops to comprehend. Enjoy a short reprieve and listen to some U2 for a couple of moments before proceeding onward. I propose the melody "Vertigo."

Daily Campaign Budget

Feel good? Now that we understand the two methods which determine how the daily budget of each campaign is set up, we need to examine how the total daily budgets of all campaigns work against the daily spending limit of Facebook.
Remind yourself what that means. Each campaign has a daily budget to spend, which you set. Facebook also sets a limit for daily spending across the account. Simply stated, while it is possible to create ads with regular budgets that add up to more than the daily spending limit of Facebook, the entire campaign will be shut down at the daily spending limit irrespective of how much daily budget is left in any campaign. Was it? Read that sentence a few times, again.

Assume that there are two campaigns, each set at a limit of $50 per day. The daily limits of each campaign will be spent down at whatever rates the ads are clicked on. This isn't likely to happen equally between campaigns. Use round numbers to explain quickly if Campaign 1 is spending $30 and Campaign 2 is spending $20, then the automatic $50-per-day cap would shut down the account until the next day. This is a double-edged sword, because the regular account-wide cap does a nice job controlling campaign spending. On the other hand, it's a bummer with a default limit, as we usually want to spend more than 50 bucks in a single day.

The issue is that if one campaign races out of the gate and the campaign cap is set too high, the other campaigns (which by their very nature will be going slow because they're smaller segments) may not get an airing. The alternative is to start with lower daily campaign sums by splitting out media spending more equally to figure out which campaigns will spend faster. Then, once you have run the account for a couple of days, start making adjustments based on knowledge of how each campaign performs. Some campaigns should spend faster because the segments are bigger, while other campaigns will move more slowly with smaller segments.

Interestingly enough, Facebook defaults on the daily budget of each campaign to $50 although the total daily spending on the account is limited to $50. This can result in injuries. For example, if Campaigns 1, 2, 3, and 4 are left at the default daily budget of $50 and the account-wide limit of $1,000 is set, the account will spend $200 before you wake up. If you have a Facebook representative, be careful not to increase the daily spending too much, because then there is a risk that the entire account will spend to the campaign level.

The bottom line of setting the budget is as follows:

If Facebook isn't going to increase the spending limit and you don't have enough cash to test all of your campaigns, then consider rolling out the campaigns one at a time to test how quickly each spends. Basically the only way to know for sure how much a company can invest each day is to test each campaign. Once you understand each campaign, holistic budgeting across all campaigns becomes easier.

Regardless of how big a daily limit is, regulate the growth of the account at the level of the campaign. Use the lifetime spending environment to ensure there are no injuries.

Be conscious, for various reasons, that campaigns are spending at different rates, slower or faster. These include the size of the page, how good your advertisements are and how much you're bidding. Beware of the default campaign limit of $50. They don't care when the account limitation is small, but if Facebook raises the restrictions on daily spending when you're not watching, like on a weekend (which happens), and there are loads of ads, you have to anticipate unnecessary spending.

Sure, we're nitty-gritty through, but there's still more to go. For this next section choose whatever music you enjoy. That is going to make a difference.

Creating offers

The campaigns keep one or more advertisements to check, and each campaign has a daily budget. Every ad within a campaign contains a copy, a picture, a target and a bid. Bids are set at the ad level, and can be manipulated either for each ad and/or at the campaign overview level within the creation / editing process. Facebook Ads is an auction model, meaning advertisers are bidding against other advertisers who are competing for the same real-estate on-screen. Facebook is prepared to bill your credit card using two options to choose from at the individual ad level: CPC (cost per click) or CPM (cost per 1,000 impressions). There's also a "quality score" for each ad that includes several FB monitor signals, including CTR, users who click on the little "X" to say they don't like the ad, and other factors. The position of the ad on the page, higher or lower on the sidebar to the right, is most likely determined as follows: bid + quality score (qScore)= ad position. That's familiar turf to you AdWords PPC jockeys.

Facebook tends to measure the quality score that includes the Effective CPC (eCPC) whether the ad is CPC or CPM bid. What you need to know at this point is that, regardless of the billing model, the FB algorithm pushes away from continuously displaying ads that no one clicks upon.

A standard test method is to run identical ads, alternating CPM versus CPC. Such tests are the only real way of telling what's relevant to your campaign, ads, bids, social segment competitiveness, and other factors.

The most important takeaway is that it's not the bid alone that sets the location of your ad in relation to the other ads. It is bid combination with qScore. Bid + score for consistency (qScore)= ad location. As for the strategy of bidding, Facebook suggests bids in the ad UI at two different points (which are not fully synchronized). The bid is set automatically after an ad has been made, right below the targeting information and next to where you decide in which campaign the ad will be in. Of course you can edit this preset bid. Usually the initial bid is about the center of the bid range which is proposed later in the campaign app. Practice has shown us that, as shown by CTR, bidding to the highest suggested amount gets premium placement. The ads are low-cost enough to be cheap on initial launch. In reality, your quality score seems to be influenced by a weak CTR, which will influence the cost of that ad in future. Later in this chapter we're going to look at different methods to sharpen the bid to be more effective.

There is no formal way to correlate the bid to the position where the ad appears on the page (rank), or if the ad appears at all. That isn't to say you can't work out where your ad will be put in relation to your bid. The workaround is simple. Go to your own Facebook profile, and add to your marketing interests. Although it's a far-from-perfect solution, the ranking of the ads that show should give some indication of the competition for that social segment as well as the ad ranking in relation to the bid.

Change the offer, and see the effect. If it appears other, more dominant interests in your Facebook profile are having too much impact on the ads, just remove the other interests, at least temporarily. Try to adjust the bids, and take note of any change in placement. As a word of caution, for a while, there were some rogue devices out there that scraped within Facebook to expose social segment ad rankings. Facebook has demonstrated a propensity to sue people for such activity. If you're a grey-hat marketer, and your technique of choice is data extraction, be advised.

Another classic way to figure out what bid is actually needed is to start high and slowly back down the bids, all the while noticing the changes in traffic. Not doing this in the other direction is vitally important. Facebook isn't saying exactly what its qScore is, but there's certainly a component that recognizes which ads don't receive clicks. It is probable that the qScore takes into consideration the position of the ad. The platform, however, is too young for us to trust this algorithm which was designed to make more money for Facebook. We would always rather start by giving Facebook money "like" our ad (pun intended) and then gradually scale off the bids back. Our experience tells us that the results are not as good as starting high if we start low and move higher. It is always better to first give money to Facebook. Consider it "buying your way into the auction." As mentioned above, Facebook Ads have two basic bidding models: cost per click (CPC) and cost per thousand impressions (CPM). Some advertisers swear by one of the two models but nowadays conventional wisdom seems to be skewing towards CPC. The ranking of the ad is contingent on the bid and the quality score in both biding models. At this point, the minimum CPC is $.01. The minimum current CPM is set at $.02. For CPC and CPM the minimum daily budget is $1.00. Therefore, the budget must be at least twice the CPC or CPM that you listed. So if you're designating a CPC of $8.00 then the daily budget must be at least $16.00.

Cost-per-Click (CPC) Model

In the cost-per-click model, advertisers are never charged

anything more than the entered maximum bid, but the amount charged per click (CPC) is usually less. For example, if you bid for an ad for $1.10 CPC, you're telling FB that you're willing to spend up to $1.10 a click away. But if the system determines that your ad can "win the auction" by bidding only $.80 to claim the next highest position, you'll only be charged $.80 for that click. One reason we love cost per click is that it doesn't charge for all impressions not clicked on. The other way to think of the cost per click is no cost to no clicks! I really don't want to pay for impressions that don't result in traffic in a paradigm where hundreds of millions of impressions are common in a campaign. Consider not clicking on these extra impressions as free branding that dilutes the CPM inside the CPC model.

You have to have your average CPC lower than the daily budget. The average spending must be at least double the CPC that you have stipulated. Every day the total cost of the clicks will never exceed your daily budget.

Cost-per-Impression (CPM) Model

The other bidding model, CPM, is where advertisers are charged for every thousand impressions displayed regardless of whether users are clicking or not. Facebook preaches, "As a CPM advertiser, you're finding out that it's more relevant for many people to see your ad, not necessarily to take action after seeing your ad. CPM advertisement is usually more effective for advertisers wanting to raise visibility of their brand or product, whereas CPC advertising is more effective for advertisers hoping for a certain answer from users (such as purchases or registration). "It has not always been our experience that CPM is less costly for branding assignments, as compared to the clever use of CPC. Research alone will say. The bottom line of CPM is that you are invoiced for prints.

In addition, brand advertisers should test the CPC model, undertaking tactics whereby the ad copy limits the CTR. Instead, all impressions not clicked are free. Refer to the "The Five Levels of Brand Clarity" section of the previous chapter for more context. CPC bidding and ad copy modeling are the methods for the crafty marketer to pay for just a few clicks while keeping the CPM extremely low.

Your average budget needs to be less than your full CPC or CPM. Your daily budget must be at least twice the CPC or CPM that you have set. The total cost of everyday clicks or impressions will never go beyond your daily budget.

Facebook also offers another option, finally: using Suggested Bid (Simple Mode). Simply select this option positions your bid in the middle of the suggested bid range in Set a Different Bid (Advanced Mode) which is how the default UI is set. Facebook does not document whether Simple Mode scales the bid up or down in the pack automatically as other advertisers bid higher or lower.

Note: The really big issue for advanced users when deciding between CPC and CPM is your eCPM (effective cost per thousand impressions) or eCPC (effective cost per click) for both CPC and CPM. Based on what the advertiser wants to optimize, one will be more economical.

There is no formal way to compare the bid to the place where the ad appears on the page (rank), or if the ad appears at all. That isn't to say you can't work out where your ad will be put in relation to your bid. The workaround is simple. Go to your own Facebook profile, and add to your marketing preferences. Although it's a far-from-perfect solution, the ranking of the ads that show should give some indication of the competition for that social segment as well as the ad ranking in relation to the bid.

Adjust the offer, and see the impact. If it seems other, more powerful interests in your Facebook profile are having too much effect on the advertising, just delete the other interests, at least temporarily. Try to adjust the bids, and take note of any change in placement. As a word of caution, for a while, there were some rogue tools out there that scraped within Facebook to expose social segment ad rankings. Facebook has shown a tendency to sue people for such behavior. If you're a grey-hat marketer, and your technique of choice is data extraction, be advised.

Another classic way to figure out what bid is actually needed is to start high and slowly back down the bids, all the while noticing the changes in traffic. Not doing this in the other direction is vitally important. Facebook isn't saying exactly what its qScore is, but there's definitely an aspect that recognizes which ads don't receive clicks. It is probable that the qScore takes into consideration the position of the ad. The website, however, is too young for us to trust this algorithm which was designed to make more money for Facebook. We would always rather start by giving Facebook money "like" our ad (pun intended) and then gradually scale off the bids back. Our experience tells us that the results are not as good as starting high if we start low and move higher. It is always better to first give money to Facebook. Consider it "buying your way into the auction." As mentioned above, Facebook Ads have two basic bidding models: cost per click (CPC) and cost per thousand impressions (CPM). Many advertisers swear by one of the two models but nowadays conventional wisdom seems to be skewing towards CPC. The rating of the ad is based on the bid and the price score in both biding models. At this point, the minimum CPC is $.01. The minimum existing CPM is set at $.02. For CPC and CPM the minimum daily budget is $1.00. Additionally, your budget must be at least twice the CPC or CPM that you specified. So if you're designating a CPC of $8.00 then the regular budget must be at least $16.00.

Cost-per-Click (CPC) model

Advertisers are never paid more than the overall bid entered in the cost-per-click scheme, but typically the amount charged per click (CPC) is lower. For example, if you bid for an ad for $1.10 CPC, you're telling FB that you're willing to spend up to $1.10 a click away. But if the system determines that your ad can "win the auction" by bidding only $.80 to claim the next highest position, you'll only be charged $.80 for that click. One reason we love cost per click is that it doesn't bill for all interactions not clicked on. The other way to think of the cost per click is no cost to no clicks! I really don't want to pay for impressions that don't result in traffic in a system where hundreds of millions of impressions are popular in a campaign. Consider not clicking on these extra impressions as free branding that dilutes the CPM inside the CPC model.

You have to have the average CPC lower than the daily budget. Your average budget must be at least twice the CPC that you have stipulated. Every day the total cost of the clicks will never surpass your daily budget.

Cost-per-Impression (CPM) Model

The other bidding technique, CPM, is where advertisers are paid for every thousand impressions seen irrespective of whether or not users click. Facebook preaches, "As a CPM advertiser, you're finding out that it's more relevant for many people to see your ad, not necessarily to take action after seeing your ad. CPM advertisement is usually more effective for advertisers wanting to raise visibility of their brand or product, whereas CPC advertising is more effective for advertisers hoping for a certain answer from users (such as purchases or registration). "It has not always been our experience that CPM is less costly for branding assignments, as compared to the clever use of CPC. Research alone will say. The bottom line of CPM is that you are invoiced for prints.

In addition, brand marketers will test the CPC model, pursuing strategies whereby the ad copy restricts the CTR. Instead, all impressions not clicked are free. Refer to the "The Five Levels of Brand Clarity" section of the previous chapter for more context. CPC bidding and ad copy modeling are the tools for the crafty marketer to pay for just a few clicks while keeping the CPM extremely low.

Your average budget needs to be less than your full CPC or CPM. Your daily budget must be at least twice the CPC or CPM that you have set. The total cost of everyday clicks or impressions will never go beyond the daily budget.

Facebook also offers another option, finally: using Suggested Bid (Simple Mode). Simply select this option positions your bid in the middle of the suggested bid range in Set a Different Bid (Advanced Mode) which is how the default UI is set. Facebook does not document whether Simple Mode scales the bid up or down in the pack automatically as other advertisers bid higher or lower.

Note: The really big issue for advanced users when choosing between CPC and CPM is your eCPM (effective cost per thousand impressions) or eCPC (effective cost per click) for both CPC and CPM. Depending on what the advertiser needs to maximize, one will be more economical.

CHAPTER EIGHT

Facebook Advertising Hacks to Generate High-Ticket Sales

What Is a High Ticket Item?

So I will clarify what I mean by a High Ticket Product or Service to kick things off. This is normally a product or service that has a healthy margin attached to it; over $100 for products and generally over $1000 for services. An important note to make now is that this profit within the initial sale does not need to be made. If your customers ' average lifetime value is around these figures then you're also perfectly positioned to get the most out of Facebook Advertising, however, there may be a time when you're waiting to recover some of the upfront cost of buying a customer.

What Advertising for High Ticket Items on Facebook?

So why are those organizations so well suited to use Facebook

Ads? Simply put—it's because you can afford to spend more on acquiring a customer per Lead or Sale in the form of cost. This takes multiple meetings between the company and the customer to push someone through the purchasing process, from first being aware of a product or service to contemplating the purchase, to actually taking action. These interactions need to be managed through a smart, strategic mix of content and marketing messages that move a prospect through this process, building momentum toward buying as you go. The higher the value of that sale, the greater you can invest in ensuring that prospects are effectively and on a scale moved through this process.

How to Attract Clients at High End?

High-ticket sales need top-end customers. Although attracting more customers will always be a significant pillar of business, acquiring the right type of customer is much more effective in moving higher-priced goods and services. Attracting high-end customers not only leads to better productivity, but also to a more dedicated customer/business relationship, a higher value for the client and a greater impact. The problem in order to make high-ticket sales should not be whether to make high-end customers your target audience but how to catch their attention.

Hacks for High-Ticket Facebook Advertising.

Hack #1. Storytelling

Three billion user accounts were breached in 2016. About a portion of American adults has had their personal information taken. Cybercrime has grown three times in a little more than a year.

These stats never implied a lot to me. Naivety and numbness are likely.

Until I saw this "Threats of Free WiFi" infographic from ExpressVPN. That provoked my curiosity. Never even thought about air terminal or lodging connections. So I delved further into Man in the center attacks. Presently, I'm composing this in a lodging entryway with a – you got it – VPN connected.

That is the means by which it works. That is the manner by which we discover things on the web. Especially on Facebook.

I didn't go looking for a VPN. I never realized I required one in any case. I didn't esteem it, consequently, I didn't search for it.

Instead, it discovered me. Luck.

All gratitude to an arbitrary infographic. Content.

This equivalent careful process even applies to B2B companies. But, not actually as fast.

~Fifteen years prior I read Permission Marketing. Was still in college. "This fella is smart," I thought.

~Ten years prior I read Inbound Marketing. (Distinctive title, same reason.) "These HubSpot people are smart," I thought.

~Three+ years back I turned into a HubSpot client, forking over ~$10k/year.

~Two+ years prior. At that point a HubSpot Partner. Getting others to fork over $10k/year.

An overnight client evangelist. Ten to fifteen years really taking shape. All starting with content. In any case, more specifically, worth and instruction around a specific torment point.

Inbound marketing software wasn't on my radar ten years prior. (Nor was it in my budget.) Instead, building a profession in marketing and utilizing innovation to get clients, was.

So there, you start.

An interesting story. A story. A clever snare that attracts people.

Hack #2. Content Mapping

Vegas. Dingy club. Mid-nineties.

One speculator looks for advice from another. Step by step instructions to make the most cash at all amount of time. Pokers the game.

"They're called 'marks'. The people who aren't in the same class as you. They're who you need."

"However, how would you find them?"

"Here. I'll show you."

The veteran card shark accomplishes something under the table. Directly before 'racking a shotgun'. It echoes noisily.
A couple of pivots, seeing the well-known clamor.

"Those are the ones you don't have any desire to play with," commented the vet. "Everyone else is your imprint."

This remarkable scene comes the kindness of Perry Marshall in his splendid 80/20 Sales and Marketing. He calls it 'racking the shotgun' (for evident reasons). The point is to utilize marketing endeavors to inspire a reaction. They ought to get a couple of people to react. What's more, that should assist you with making sense of the ones to concentrate on (and which to overlook).

Various types of content appeal to various people. Various topics and diverse key terms additionally do, as well. Content mapping is the process of coordinating the secret sauce to the opportune people.

Hack #3. Interest Intersection and Exclusions

All content mapped offers should target custom audiences like past leads or ongoing site visits.

However, how would you target those people?

You know storytelling gets them. Content mapping sustains them. Be that as it may, how would you find them in any case?

Preferably, you need an audience size of in any event 500,000 to one million. Excessively small and campaigns can't enhance. Excessively huge and you're going to squander cash on irrelevant guests.

The problem is that connecting "Software" as interest is excessively conventional. Millions and millions may follow a solitary media distribution, so they're out, as well.

Instead, you need a sensitive exercise in careful control of interests (regardless of whether that is media-based substances, influencers, different companies, work titles, and so on.) with the correct socioeconomics (so under 30, no budget, while over 50 and they don't 'get it').

However. Excluding people is practically more significant than fitting the bill for service companies.

So exclusions not just assist you with throttling back audience size to hit that enchantment extend. In any case, more significantly, it permits you to dispense with people, callings, enterprises, or advancement levels that won't be a solid match.

Easy model.

You need to sell marketing and advertising services. Your clients need enough information so as to comprehend what you do and why it's significant. However, they can't be learned to the point that they're already doing it for themselves.

Targeting other service suppliers or management advisors is a decent start.

Adding in a layer of those people who read Inc. or on the other hand Fast Company is even better since you can figure that they're relatively educated.

Yet, at that point barring ad agencies and marketing agencies is a sure thing since they already do what you're attempting to sell.

Hack #4. Micro-Conversions

One-and-done will be done.

Complex sales are frequently long and drawn out. This means you have to cut up your sustaining (and desires) in like manner into micro-conversions that gradually move people closer to purchasing.

Think eBook downloads, contextual analysis pageviews, the quantity of visits over the previous thirty days, and that's only the tip of the iceberg. These smaller than usual commitments or delicate objectives move people through your funnel, even if it's not appearing as another Goal in Google Analytics.

Take, for instance, recordings.

They're universally loved. Stats never observed a video that they didn't care for.

Presentation page conversions soar. Watchers buy more. Executives make a move.

Which makes video sees the ideal micro-conversion. Picture great, truly. Since based on pretty much every detail ever, the video sees lead to more buys.

The difficulty, obviously, is following, estimating, and demonstrating how these delicate 'center of the funnel' actions lead straightforwardly to the conversion event days or weeks after the fact.

That is, troublesome in case you're not utilizing the correct apparatus.

HubSpot's lead scoring can assist you with following 'unequivocal' or hard conversions, yet additionally those gentler, 'certain' micro ones like pageviews, specific page visits (for example Plans and Pricing), and that's only the tip of the iceberg.

Hack #5. Ad Placements

Desktop News Feed ads are the best.

Problem is, they're additionally the most expensive.

You can extend ad dollars without yielding outcomes by utilizing the correct ad placements at the ideal time. Here's a speedy look.

Step #1. Need Cheap Visits? Start with Mobile.

Financial matters 101.

Less interest + more inventory = lower costs.

Two additional advantages.

The first is purchaser conduct. Our CEO Massimo stated, "Users will discover your product on their telephones… at that point buy it the following day on their desktop."

The second is that Facebook as of late unveiled custom audiences based on Facebook engagement. This means you can start building custom audiences with storytelling to target specific groups of people (utilizing interest incorporations and exclusions), all without those people ever having to really leave Facebook.

Facebook's AMP-like Instant Articles is your first option.

Step #2. Retargeting Custom Audiences? Utilize the Right Sidebar.

Right-hand sidebar ads are small. Too small.

The image isn't sufficiently large to convey something confounded or nitty-gritty. There's scarcely enough space for a couple of headline words. Furthermore, there's unquestionably insufficient space for a portrayal to add context.

Taking a Desktop News Feed ad and driving it into the correct sidebar just makes problems. Since the stuff is obscured. Gets shortened. Or then again unintelligible.
There is one exemption, however.

Brand awareness.

Utilizing right sidebar ads for retargeting endeavors to people who already notice what your identity is and what you offer can deliver more affordable outcomes.

Step #3. Ready to Generate Sales? Go with the Desktop News Feed
To wrap things up, depending on the longer-than-common text

and bigger than-regular image to persuade, coax, and produce conversion actions.

Or then again use Carousel ads to do that times two, three, or four diverse worth props.

Hack #6. Develop a Follow Up Process

Complex sales take longer. Dozens of 'contacts' before purchasing whatnot. (Have you heard this already?)

You're leading people on from micro-conversion to micro-conversion. Gradually moving them through the center of the funnel until they're ready, voluntarily, to plunk down and discuss work.

Incentives can assist you with moving this along. Like the carrot out in front that gets people to continue going toward your decision.

Product companies have it easy here. Slap on a 10% off or BOGO arrangement and call it a day. Mayhem follows.

Service companies don't have it so easy. Limiting and value breaks just debase your offering and take steps to dissolve validity (not to mention already razor-slight net revenues) in the long-term. (Recollect that entire positioning piece?)

Instead, service companies have to go with exclusive content or some need access to keep people moving.

Hack #7. Make it Easy to Buy

Adding itemized plans and valuing help make the product offering concrete and unmistakable for buyers.

Online lead gen is extreme. It requires some additional exertion. Furthermore, the 'Free Consultation' page motivates or educates nobody.

Your offer is the one thing isolating 2% conversions with those topping 10%, as indicated by $3 billion+ in yearly ad spend investigated by WordStream.

Leading pointers matter, sure. In any case, that is not why people buy services by the day's end. They're doing it since they see a superior future coming up. One whose long-term incentive far exceeds the momentary costs.

CHAPTER NINE

Landing Page Considerations

The user determines to target. The ad is imaginative, it makes a promise to copy and image. The landing page must genuinely welcome the customer, affirm their click-through decision and funnel toward conversion. This triumvirate, when properly executed, is the mystical series that successful marketers exploit to KPI sales in systematic herding of consumers.

By clicking on an ad (and therefore its underlying URL) the landing page is the web destination users are routed to. The decisions regarding where users are sent are based on two key factors. Secondly, landing pages should be based on the marketing targets at hand. Second, the Facebook Ad Guidelines include a set of persnickety guidelines. Check the FB Support section to find "Publicity Guidelines." Many landing pages have lead generation forms in them, and others have descriptions of a product with a Buy Now button. White-paper updates and event signups are displayed on landing pages. The landing page is the tool for the conversion of the traffic generated from FB ads.

Experienced marketers understand how important conversion is to the consistency of the landing page. I can't tell you how many times I have heard people say Facebook ads aren't working... but their landing page is bad. If you're concerned about conversion, landing pages will make Facebook ads either look really good or really bad. Marketers who are good at targeting and writing ads can drive clicks until the cows come home, dump mass traffic to an audience all day, but whether or not those converting users probably have more to do with the landing page than anything else.

In the real world, it is a lot the same if you think about it. Say you are walking in the food court of the mall hungry but unsure about what to eat. For all food-court vendors, you are a fertile option because you are a hungry human looking to food in the market. A bright sign for beefy, succulent hot dogs from Coney Island catches your eye but as you enter the stand, the only wieners on the menu are made of pink braised tofu. The real destination had failed to keep the promotional promise. There's a pretty good chance you'll turn away from finding some real beef, so obviously, the conversion rate for the tofu dog vendor will suffer because of the lack of promise to keep. The pages in which land is the same way.

In a vacuum, your landing page doesn't exist. It works hand in hand with targeted demographics and creative ads. That's why any discussion of landing pages includes targeting and innovation, the magic mustard which first powered the press. Search PPC professionals have been serving pages contextually designed to lift landing page conversion for keywords since the' 90s. Now that Facebook allows overfocused targeting based on personal preferences, shrewd advertisers realize that with the right socially sensitive landing page, the predilections of the audience can be further leveraged.

Let's research how the creative ad could influence elements of the landing page. To Facebook users who have clicked because they are interested in "Nikon hunting official," routing users to a beautiful Nikon Buckmasters product page makes perfect sense. If the headline of the ad says, "Take the Big Buck," then it might work to have the headline of the landing page be, "Bag the Big Buck! Nikon Buckmasters. "Subtle differences are equally important. Users who clicked because of a "university" interest may respond more enthusiastically to pictures of students walking outside ivy-covered campus buildings than those interested in "music college," who may react to tight shots of undergraduates playing guitars in the student-union buildings. Only testing those theories will tell you definitively.

Reinforcing the targeting criteria which incentivized the click as text and/or salient images on the landing page is generally accepted as best practice. Furthermore, on the landing page, the text, look and feel should be congruent in definition, message and vernacular to the title and body copy of the commercial. Multivariate landing page testing is important, which means experimenting with different combinations of social segments, ad copy, and landing page before KPI conversion is optimized. We call the targeting/ad message/page landing testing multivariate.

Facebook Ads landing pages can be easily designed to resonate on a much deeper, personal level. That's because other elements in the targeting grid may be enhanced for landing page leverage in addition to the basic targeting elements (geographic location, ad copy definition, and time of day). Just think of the groovy possibilities expressed in the gender, race, interests, employment, job, age, sexuality, relationship status and other social graphic elements dependent on landing page customization.

The degree to which you can configure landing pages depends on how dramatically the marketer splits segments into smaller, more oriented buckets. Let's presume we're making super-stylized iPad security cases and want to sell to everyone in the U.S. as well as English speakers abroad. While lumping all iPad users into one huge bucket, let's divide those users by age, gender, and venue. A successful landing page starts with focused segmentation. Let's look at how the targeting buckets will look segmented.

We now have a little bit more segmentation in version B of the Estimated Reach stack. Knowing we're aiming at men means we can customize things a little bit more. Maybe the landing page will show the big muscles of a hot lady or of a dude. Consider the effect of different background colors, font choices, and copy density depending on targeting variables and the copy's simplicity or complexity. Knowing that we're dealing with people will help focus to test the entire look, feel and content of landing pages.

Version C shows the same considerations as B, only for females.

Stuff in version D gets more specific. This age group is aimed at 17 and younger males. The youngest user on Facebook is aged 13. Make fun of Justin Bieber and Hannah Montana, expose an iPad to a pretty 15-year-old girl or invoke teenage-boy stuff elsewhere. Keep in mind the word vernacular; use words like dude, OMG, and LMAO in your ads. Usually, the Facebook editorial lets us get away with body copy colloquialisms, though maybe not headlines. Integrate the landing page closely by amplifying the verbiage of the ad's colloquiality on the landing page.

Version E is quite interesting because it's all the old guys (like me) on iPads. If you're selling sex, perhaps make it a mature-looking 35-year-old lady. Display an iPad within that age group in a man's hands. Grown-ups appear to be more responsible than children on average, so try pushing the buttons in the ad copy to "protect your prized iPad investment."

Version F shows 1,460 gay women in Canada or the United States are identified on Facebook. Be assertive. Show people pictured holding hands or kissing with an iPad. As mentioned earlier in the book, segments of the homosexual market tend to have more cash that can be disposed of, so even though this group is smaller, you might have good luck. Evaluate gay websites like Advocate.com and OutTraveler.com for image templates, vernacular text, color trends and other innovative variables as input into how the gay-focused landing page fits in.

The segment is shown in version G targets people from the Midwest to the East Coast, between 24 and 38 live in the northern United States. Maybe set the scene at the ski hill during winter months. Show an extremely cold lady in Cancun dreaming of a hot guy with an iPad. Find emotional buttons for that demographic.

Drive them over.

Version H is a micro-segment that targets intensively university students at a scientific level. Perhaps that means technical language on the landing page in the advertisements and pictures of the lab coats. Seek quirky permutations in the headlines and body copy of classic formula syntax. You know who those are. Make the most of that information.

Finally, the edition I shows all married men who speak English and live in countries other than the USA. Draw a bead on those consumers from Hong Kong to Austria. Joke about sharing the iPad with their wives, or not. Perhaps selling them on the protection, "If you're going to share it with the wife...." It might be useful to portray couples so that the users feel acclimatized.

CHAPTER TEN

Dynamic Landing Pages, Tagging, and Conversion Tracking

There are two elements that are essential for a good return on investment (ROI): the ability to build landing pages with creative elements that configure automatically based on what ad was clicked on Conversion tracking to determine whether or not certain ad/landing page combinations yield sweet KPI fruit This speaks to techniques that advanced marketers have used for years to sharpen campaign.

The system relies on the same strategy for both dynamic external landing pages and external page conversion tracking, which includes labeling the destination URL with variables. Such tags are used to "tell" the content management system on the landing page as to how to customize the page. Web analytics often use these to generate reports that explain whether or not the landing pages translate to KPIs.

The development of gazillions of personalized landing page permutations with static HTML is just not feasible when marketing to more than a few targeting segments. Also, by some method, we will need to monitor conversion for pages outside Facebook. Easily tagging each ad with a unique set of URL variables makes those two critical needs easier. URL variables are text strings after the? In several page URLs. Most marketers are familiar with URL variables, also known as tracking tags or URL parameters, and have used them for years in searching for PPCs, emails and other online campaigns. Many marketing programs by third parties which track metrics do the same.

Let's break the example down: http:/www.aimclearblog.com?Campaign= nikon-buckmaster&headline= Bag percent 20Procent 20Big percent 20Buck&ad-id=243 Variables are introduced by question mark. One variable is concatenated by the ampersands until the end of the previous. Variables are indicated as[name variable]=[value variable].

The American Standard Code for Information Interchange (ASCII) text character is 20 percent for transmitting space (spaces are excluded in URLs).

The terms for the three variables are program, headline, and ad-id.

The value of the campaign variable is Nikon-Buckmaster.

Bag percentage 20The 20Big percent 20Buck is the headline numerical interest. Notice that we have capitalized on the words in the meaning of this variable because this text will appear on our landing page as the headline.

243 The ad-id attribute is a number.

Begin by marking of ad with these three URL variables, where the campaign is the name of the campaign, the headline is the copy headline of the desired landing page and ad-id is a unique identifier for every ad in the whole account. It's fine for different accounts to use the same headline. If you are confident, go ahead and include in the spreadsheet the name, body copy, and pictures from every ad.

Ask your friendly web developer to code a request for the headline variable from the inbound URL for dynamic landing pages that autoconfigure contextually based on URL variables, and display it as text on the page. The request also to swap the main image on the landing page (dynamic), contingent on either headline or ad-id. If that makes no sense to you, just sit down with your web developer and ask them to explain it. A deeper explanation is beyond the scope of this book but you will find the concepts very easy to digest. In their bag of tricks, almost every web developer has this basic maneuver, no matter what dynamic language your landing page is coded in—.ASP,.PHP,.JSP,.CFM, and so on.

The URL variables system serves double-duty use as conversion tracking tags to keep track of (or not) conversion at the campaign, headline, and/or unique ad-id level. Ask your analytics person to create reports that correlate traffic to a completed conversion containing these URL variables. It is really straightforward. If a user enters the dedicated "Thank You For [Converting]" page with any [variable value], then conversion has occurred.

Here are a few other considerations, many of which could be regarded as best practices: it is possible to change the variable names I used. Speak to your analytics team to ask if structured variable names are in place to serve such purposes, names that jive with the analytics platform or conversion tagging schema.

The tagging scheme is not limited to three variables, by any means.

The headline idea behind using a percent 20 is to use a database to get around and keep the dynamic landing page, which is actually a small application, easy. Another common method of naming a database record is to use only the unique ad-id, which can contain any number of page elements.

Users may connect from blogs or websites to those pages. To prevent duplicate content as it relates to search engine optimization (SEO), it is strongly suggested that PPC devote such landing pages. Stop them from being indexed organically by search engines using meta no-index no-follow on the website, which is a robots.txt entry preventing bots from indexing the sites, and also by having no index no-follow any links within the web to those landing pages. If you want to have your PPC landing pages indexed for organic search, creating different versions is usually better.

Socializing External Landing Pages

Will direct marketers put Facebook, Twitter, YouTube and/or other social buttons on every PPC landing page as part of the template? The response seems a simple yes at first glance. "Socialize everything, of course," you shout,! After all, these days the Net isn't all about social media? "The lack of all-powerful and pervasive social media like-me-now buttons, how could it be right?

Nonetheless, consider the results. Other than those leading users down the conversion funnel, providing options on a landing page can bleed and spray the traffic away from the conversion. In addition to the conversion path, we have studied many outbound-click maps for landing pages which offered users various options. Many consumers, who might otherwise have converted, would completely forsake the social click commercial funnel.

If the KPI is a direct response practice, we frequently advise clients to relegate "being social" as the secondary KPI, reduced in graphic weight as long as testing shows it is not distracting from the primary conversion. In such cases, I would prefer to put the features of socialization on the Thank-you tab. Sure, sacrificing sales for happy social friends often makes sense, but make that decision deliberate, data-driven and based on real business objectives.

For external landing pages, test enough to ensure the primary KPI is not cannibalized by the socialization features. One thing is certain: No one-size-fits-all strategy. Test the social envelope, and push it. Remember to always put consumers in a well-laid funnel, direct them toward conversion, and be careful if, for whatever reason, you break targets even to make a friend.

"Buying Fans" with Ads and Social Landing Pages You can target your own Facebook page with ads, as discussed previously in this book. Most companies are using Facebook Ads to build up their fan count and "buy followers" efficiently. Costs can be very small, and the results spectacular. We've seen hundreds or even millions of fans bought for less than pennies each. Facebook Ads can be very effective in promoting social KPIs both within Facebook and outside it. Ruminate about choices. Promoting an event organized using the events platform offered by Facebook? Consider routing clicks from announcements to the event page. The URL can be easily obtained by simply copying it from your browser and inserting it into your ad. Facebook ads are great to support other social KPIs on Facebook, such as getting users to like a company page, downloading a Facebook app, viewing videos, joining groups and even jumping into a provocative dialogue. Within Facebook media landing pages are the current trend in a world where "Ls" matter and user engagement is the new black.

Also referred to as "buying friends," it is perhaps the most omnipresent method to send users who click on ads to fan pages, or other Facebook profile pages. We've seen trendy guerrilla advertisers, motivation users, to like pages for as few as pennies per se, signing up thousands or even hundreds of thousands of users. I personally love the acquired "Cost per Fan" (CPF) measurement. The classic play is to provide Facebook users with attractive content, but only if they've liked your post. Try posting fan-only exclusive deals, premium content, the inside track foreshadowing a future product creation, or exclusive access to inside knowledge about a celebrity.

Offer users had anticipated the release of white papers to the general public, again, only if they like the page. There is literally sprouting up a cottage industry where third-party Facebook Ads production companies offer friend purchase packages charging by the friend. As with most lead-generation third-party providers, doing so on your own might well be less costly. In crafting the pitch, be the most creative kid on the block and not be spammy. About buying friends: our experience has been that sometimes purchased friends aren't authentic because they don't participate much or stay around after the initial incentive has worn off. That being said, many times buying friends is a great tactic to help people find pages on which they should be connected. This depends upon the pitch and the consistency of the thought of the marketer. Getting users to like a page with an offer is quite different from being a good friend back and keeping the long haul over your new peeps.

Another natural fit for marketers on Facebook Ads is Facebook apps. Fostering an organic food authenticity calculator app for moms and dads interested in organic food, sustainable farming, wellness for children and other associated affinities is a no-brainer. Selling downloads of game apps is super-easy when selling to Facebook users who are fanatically interested in Farmville and other games that are extremely popular. Consider selling to users interested in Mensa, Rubik's Cube or the popular board game Mastermind a human memory software program. Like all ads on Facebook Ads, the Tao lies in the relationship between targeting, ad creative and how easily you welcome users on the landing page.

Within Facebook, sending users to landing pages has some really fun viral possibilities. After hitting a social KPI, the newly converted consumer is effectively a retransmitting tool for the cause of the marketer. Normally friends of the user will show the activities of their pal in their news feed. Since users are on Facebook, a crypt where sharing is the main focus, the sponsored content is quickly trafficked from user to user, which is a common result. It, of course, actually dilutes the CPA because you only pay for the click that takes the original converted user with you, while the friends of the user cost nothing. We've seen viral waves ripple out from in-Facebook landing pages, as user communities engage with great content around them. If that doesn't actually happen, it's sometimes a good indication that the material isn't worthy. We often use Facebook Ads for this reason to judge the potential virality of content. Remember we send users, pre-qualified by what we already know they are interested in.

Social pages that land outside Facebook can be truly effective. In reality, when we're hired to organically promote YouTube videos, we usually test the viral proclivity of the videos by sending super-focused, paying Facebook traffic to the YouTube videos. It does seem like sorcery sometimes. Users thumb up / down the video on YouTube after turning on the FB advertisements, posting on it and sharing the connection with others... or not. Promote Facebook Ads blog posts, Twitter feeds, Flickr photographs and socialized trade sites.

Of course, using your own company's website as the host domain for Facebook Ads campaign landing pages is almost always a defensible option. This is where advertisers have maximum control. If the advertisement is for a large corporation not ceding marketers access to the mothership website, suggest marketing to a subdomain you can monitor. As we will cover in more depth in the next chapter, there are definite conversion-tracking problems when using landing pages outside of your technological control within Twitter, YouTube, and other sites.

Also, because of possible viral consequences, the conversion tracking compromise is worthwhile. It's still a trade-off.

Final Prelaunch Checklist

Now, we're rock-ready. Let's make sure that everything is in place: review your payment options and ensure that the source of the billing is set up as you wish.

Facebook will restrict you with a daily limit of $50 to spend. If you need to spend more from the get-go contact Facebook.

Set the cap on lifetime spending, if you choose so.

Set the daily budget of each campaign, or ensure that its lifetime budget and schedule are set as you like.

Go through each ad, confirm it's set up as a CPC or CPM, and make sure the bid is within the budget in range and comfortably.

Determine the landing page of each ad, by market segment. If you are marketing to an external landing page, double-check that the tracking tags are in place according to the syntax of your spreadsheet and that the landing pages are dynamically configured as intended.

Adjust the budgets of your campaign, so that there is room for spending ads. If the daily limit put on Facebook is too high, and Facebook won't change it, consider starting fewer campaigns.

Verify that your tracking tag syntax has actually been tested by the analytics team to prove that conversion tracking is in place.

Any degree of unpausing: accounts, promotions, and advertising.

Fantastic! You worked your ass off and the marketing game for Facebook ads is on!

CONCLUSION

We live in a golden age of contextual target redness. As thrilling as it may be, seasoned online marketers know that the only thing that really remains the same is that absolutely nothing remains the same. Just look at what used to be monolithic Internet icons like Netscape, AOL, Yahoo! Search, and Myspace. It seemed as if things would go on forever during the height of their successes as users adopted the channels and flocked in massive droves. Time has shown us that even the most powerful Goliaths of the Internet are not impervious to the relentless march and whims of flighty users of technology.

Sure, it seems like Facebook is strong, really strong. But is it realistic to think the dominant social network will exist in perpetuity? Will Facebook, in 30 years, be the daily destination for the majority of online users on our planet? Perhaps, but probably not... What's really significant about Facebook is that it was first to launch a forward-thinking advertisement tool based on social graph data points— which turns out to be doing an awesome job of profiling individuals. In 2007 the targeting technologies rolled out incinerated the standard of the day. Still, they do. Never before have advertisers been able to serve ads aimed at such an extraordinarily focused grid of tangible human behaviors, as advised by physical human undertakings. The accomplishment, in fact, is nothing short of anthropological. For this magical moment in time, the reach and targeting of the muscle by Facebook represent the unquestioned gold standard for contextual targeting in the new world.

What is important to marketers is that we seize the opportunity in contextual space and learn to market it. Most people I meet at online marketing conferences have never heard of AltaVista or Lycos, nor do they remember Netscape, GoTo, or Overture's early days. Many of us were cutting our teeth on those canals in the' 90s. Those outlets have long vanished from the public eye. Dude, to early adopter marketers, they were absolutely essential as we learned to navigate an incredible new paradigm known as search!

Facebook is of the same magnitude and, frankly, far more important than Facebook itself. As an industry, we are planning for what's next, mastering the principle of targeting which will last forever. Facebook and whatever channels bubble next to the surface will most likely bring to fruition full functional contextual targeting to take its rightful place next to search.

One thing is certain. Getting good at Facebook Ads now helps you ready for what's next. The contextual-targeting world also includes other potential contenders. International B2B powerhouse LinkedIn has, as of this writing, amassed more than 100 million users and is rapidly expanding. Having recently introduced the ability of advertisers in a grid of other attributes, including workplace and seniority, to target the occupations of individuals, LinkedIn Ads just got a lot more intense. One would assume that LinkedIn has the data points to further refine and expand targeting, should the occasion arise. Still, the community is one-sixth the size of Facebook and advertising can cost more than four times what CPC or CPM-based Facebook ads cost. LinkedIn is all about professional behavior, so no matter what, it's unlikely we'll ever be able to target the "whole user" as much as we can on Facebook as we can.

Google-owned YouTube has interesting options, in conjunction with Google itself. A large sample of users must perform networking and information-seeking practices to advertise to a "social graph," fill out their profiles, connect with each other and share. To be sure, the voluminous nature of users searching Google and YouTube — and engaging on YouTube — has provided Google the critical mass of data needed to create a true socio-contextual targeting platform. We are going to have to wait and see. For now, the supremacy of Facebook in the world of social-graph marketing is uncontested.

What's going to be next? The geographical context will have something to do with that for physical world businesses whose locations matter. As smartphones like BlackBerry, iPhone, and Android continue to evolve into "the norm," online communities accessed by mobile phones will mash the targeting of whole-person social graphics with a physical location and will surely offer the targeting of next-gen's social graph. Mash in group channels such as foursquare and discount websites such as Groupon or review sites such as Yelp and the possibilities are fascinating.

Social media might be built into other appliances, such as cars and fridges. Whatever the evolution, if for no other reason than the critical mass of users and a guerrilla throw-it - at-the-wall mentality, Facebook is primed to be effective. One thing is for sure, the seeds probably already exist technologically and socially for what is next, just waiting to be brought online as a reflection of real life.

The future may well be represented both in the combination of services such as those just listed and in alliances created by mergers and acquisitions and mashed with modern mobile phones. Facebook was the first real target practice any of us ever had in shooting at the social graph, no matter what is next.

Facebook could accentuate the quest behind its walled garden. Or, the deeper integration with Bing will proceed in collaboration. To many, the holy grail of demographic targeting is to assign keyword queries to the social attributes. For example, what if marketers reliably understood that 47-year-old New York Single

Men who like the New York Rangers were looking for "Rubbish removal service," while college girls in Boston who like Lady Gaga are looking for "Trash removal company"? Microsoft adCenter Labs had early tools along those lines for a long time, though it did not have the sampling needed to make the data reliable. Facebook has the means to make it possible for that future.

There will be new networks in the future, Twitter and/or others, mashing up the search, social network, and physical location to give drastic benefits to people transitioning to or from Facebook to those sites.

As this occurs, new marketing networks will be developed, offering marketers more flexibility than ever in defining and targeting segments of the market. There is no reason to wait anyway, though. My mates, you have here the future.

www.ingramcontent.com/pod-product-compliance
Lightning Source LLC
Chambersburg PA
CBHW071415150726
48000CB00001B/340